Desert Tracings

WITHDRAWN

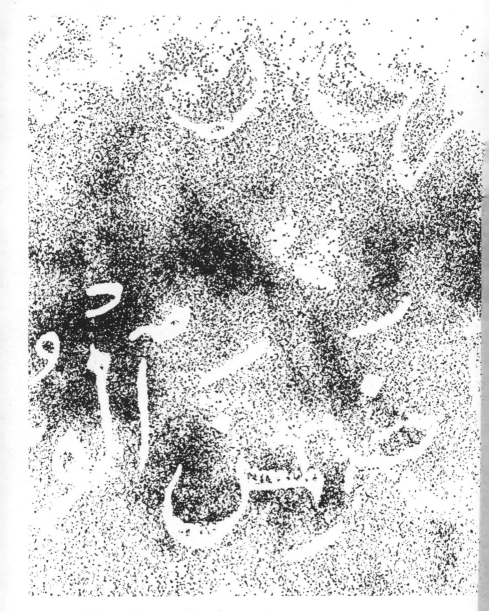

Wesleyan Poetry in Translation

Desert Tracings

Six Classic Arabian Odes
by ʿAlqama, Shánfara, Labíd, ʿAntara,
Al-Aʿsha, and Dhu al-Rúmma

Translated and Introduced by
Michael A. Sells

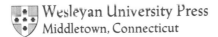

Wesleyan University Press
Middletown, Connecticut

To Janet

Introduction and translation copyright © 1989 by Michael A. Sells
Acknowledgment is given to the following journals in which translations and introductions previously appeared: *Translation* (for the journey section of the Mu‘allaqa of Labíd); *Al-‘Arabiyya* (for the translations and introductions to the odes of Shánfara and Dhu al-Rúmma).

With gratitude to the Andrew W. Mellon Foundation; the Giles Whiting Foundation; the National Endowment for the Humanities; The University of Chicago Committee on Comparative Studies in Literature and Department of Near Eastern Languages and Civilizations; Stanford University's Departments of Religious Studies, Classics, and English; and Haverford College; and to Ed Allderdice, Roger Allen, Larry Berman, John Felstiner, Elizabeth Fernea, Salma Jayyusi, Ted Good, Denise Levertov, Regan Heiserman, Th. Emil Homerin, Richard Luman, Farouk Mustapha, David Oldfather, Martin Russell, Bruce Shapiro, Ibrahim al-Sinjilawi, Richard Strier, Ruth Tonner.

Particular thanks to John Seybold, Jaroslav Stetkevych, and Suzanne Stetkevych.
Library of Congress Cataloging-in-Publication Data
Desert tracings.
   (Wesleyan poetry in translation)
   1. Arabic poetry—To 622—Translations into English.
2. English poetry—Translations from Arabic.
I. Sells, Michael Anthony. II. ‘Alqamah ibn ‘Abadah, 6th
cent. III. Series.
PJ7694.E5D3 1989   892'.1043'08   88-28084
ISBN 0-8195-2157-4
ISBN 0-8195-1158-7 (pbk.)
Manufactured in the United States of America
First Edition
Wesleyan Poetry in Translation

Contents

Desert Tracings

Introduction

The Arabian Ode

Traces of an abandoned campsite mark the beginning of the pre-Islamic Arabian ode. They announce the loss of the beloved, the spring rains, and the flowering meadows of an idealized past. Yet they also recall what is lost—both inciting its remembrance and calling it back. To hear this poetry now is to experience a similar transformation: across expanses of time and place it is a voice at once immediate and profound.

The bedouin tribes of pre-Islamic Arabia are said to have held poetry competitions during the annual fair at ʿUkáz, near Mecca. The winning poems—seven in all, according to most accounts—were embroidered in gold on rare Egyptian cloth and suspended from the ancient shrine in Mecca known as the Kaʿba. The story has been dismissed by some as an attempt to explain the puzzling name of Arabia's most famous poetry collection, the Muʿallaqát (suspended ones).[1] Yet the Legend of the Hanging Odes may offer a deeper message as a sign of cultural self-understanding. The image of the seven odes suspended from Arabia's most sacred shrine, a shrine that has since become the ritual center of Arabic culture and of the multicultural world of Islam, mirrors the generative role within the Arabic-speaking world of the Muʿallaqát and a large number of equally great poems.

Although it had labeled pre-Islamic Arabia "the Jahilíyya" (period or place of moral ignorance), Islam never abandoned the poetic heritage of that era. In the first four centuries after the founding of the new religion in 622 C.E., in cities such as Basra, Kufa, Baghdad, and Aleppo, Muslim scholars collected and preserved the oral poetic tradition of Arabia, integrating it into written culture and into the new Islamic religious sensibility. From that time the deeper patterns of the ode—if not always its formal structure—have continued to inform the Arabic literary tradition and to influence non-Arabic literatures within the world of Islam.

The origin, authorship, and transmission of this poetry, so finely developed by the time of its recording, remain a mystery. Tradition suggests that the poetry was composed by individual authors, to whom it ascribes names and biographies, and then memorized and transmitted word for word by ráwis (rhapsodes) endowed with prodigious memories.[2] More recently some have suggested, following the oral-performance

3

model developed by Homeric scholars, that the roles of the poet and *ráwi* were intertwined: the *ráwi* did not memorize precomposed poems, but, after mastering thematic, lexical, and metrical possibilities, would compose the poem in the act of performing it.[3]

Another largely oral tradition, jazz, may offer an analogy. A song evolves with each performance. The artist learns its basic contours and then, building upon a rigorous apprenticeship in the expectations and possibilities of the tradition, performs it. The richest layering of tradition combines with the most striking spontaneity. Whether composed in the act of performance or precomposed before performance, or through some combination of the two, the early Arabian poem was not—or not only— memorized. It was remembered, recalled from out of a common sensibility and a common cultural gestalt.

The ode (qasida) is a poem seldom longer than 120 lines, composed in one of several possible meters, with a single end rhyme that remains the same throughout the poem. Its most distinctive feature is its division into three major thematic movements: the *nasíb* or remembrance of the beloved, the journey, and the boast.

The qasida opens onto the abandoned campsite—traces in the sand from rain trenches and tent pegs, blackened hearthstones, ruins (*atlál*) left by the beloved's tribe. The traces are silent. Yet they invoke. As the poet stands before them the tension of this silent invocation demands release. This is the site and wellspring of the poem.

Remembrance takes a variety of forms: torrent beds paradoxically more apparent the more they are worn down; the absent beloved's night apparition (*tayf*) before the sleepless poet; the recounting of her shifting moods and affections (*ahwál*); remembrance of her departure with the women of her tribe in their richly embroidered camel litters or howdahs; the recounting of the stations (*maqamát*) of her journey away from the poet; the black wing of the crow or the sorrowful moaning of the dove; the hoariness of a poet who looks back upon a lost youth. These and other themes and subthemes recur from poem to poem, with a measured, almost ritual solemnity. Yet in each poem they acquire a new configuration according to a subtle and always newly discovered logic of sorrow. Each new realization of loss generates a new poem, with its own circumstances, undertones, personality.

What presents itself as a description of the beloved is something very different. The simile dissembles. What occurs is not so much description as it is metamorphosis. Whenever we think we have the image pinned down, it changes. The beloved's mouth might be compared to wine as fresh as a cold stream, her grace to that of a gazelle, her eyes to the eyes of a white oryx. In apparent digression the poetic voice outruns any descriptive point through the indefinite extension of the simile or through chains of similes. The images evoked—spring rains, flowing streams, flowering meadows, desert animals birthing or nursing in poses of idyllic tranquillity—are parts of a recalled wholeness. Within the dissembling simile and at odds with its explicit intent—as if the poetic voice were pulled along against its will—the archetype is re-collected, re-membered: beloved as lost garden or spring meadow.

Look again and there is no garden, only a deserted campsite. The companions, mentioned as present with the poet when the campsite was recognized as the beloved's, are gone. The poet who in the *nasíb* meditated on what he had lost, is now himself lost, beyond the margins of human community. He embarks on a journey marked by the perishing of locusts in the midday heat, the death call of the owl by night, the wasting away of the camel, the disequilibrium and terror of the mirage. As night falls, the rider's own image—the last human form—is enveloped by darkness.

The journey account can be displaced by the depiction of the rider's mount, the camel mare (*náqa*). The *náqa* can be displaced in turn by episodes involving other desert animals: the Arabian white oryx, an exquisitely graceful antelope with long, straight, cylindrical horns; the wild ass or onager, a cousin of the zebra; and the ostrich. These animals are introduced through similes likening the *náqa* to them, but again the simile dissembles. The continued extension of the simile opens onto an independent animal episode, onto a semantic and symbolic field that stretches far beyond any descriptive similarity. The associations of the oryx (beauty, grace, fragility, giving birth, the beloved) are in fact precise opposites of those of the *náqa* (strength, a quasi-elemental endurance, wasting away, tied udders, the self of the poet). Even as the simile proclaims the *náqa* to be like the oryx, it extends in apparent digression into an independent vignette, revealing a more profound set of associative polarities.

The animals are called not by name, but by epithet: "red-legged clump-wing" for the ostrich, for example, or "sheen-of-udder," "wide-of-eyes," "wild one," "flat-nosed one," for the oryx. The more central its symbolic associations, the more epithets an animal will have.[4] Unlike the English and Homeric variety (rosy-fingered dawn, wine-dark sea), the Arabic epithet has no noun. It resembles English nomenclature for birds (red-breasted nuthatch), or horses (bay, chestnut), but for each animal there are hundreds of such terms. The animal is not so much described as it is performed. A generic term like oryx and a named object of description are replaced with an almost limitless possibility of metaphorical and metonymic marks, opening the figure onto a deeply textured world of semantic and symbolic play.

When the oryx doe is surrounded by hunters, we know she will escape. In an ostrich tableau, we can expect to find the male ostrich running back to the nest. These vignettes and metaphors and similes must have been honed and selected over generations according to the bedouin aesthetic and the subtle poetic logic of the ode. They take on a totemic solidity. Yet in suppleness of allusion and in the continual expansion and deepening of epithetic and symbolic association they achieve a remarkable sense of freedom.

The transition from the journey to the ode's final movement, the boast, often takes the form of a wine song. The wine and the song of the singing girl (*qáyna*), consolations for the loss of the beloved, contain a paradox common to many traditions: the more the poet drinks, the more he proclaims how well he has forgotten the beloved, and the more he proclaims, the more he belies his proclamation. This bacchic antinomy is at the heart of the ode as a whole. However much the *nasíb* may now be left behind, remembrance of the beloved haunts the poem, guiding and controlling the poetic voice.

The dramatic center of the boast is the *náqa* sacrifice. The poet-hero slaughters his camel mare and distributes the meat through a ritual lottery (the *máysir*) played with arrow shafts. The *náqa*'s association with the self of the poet is made explicit in the practice, mentioned in the boast, of the tying of his riding camel to the grave of the fallen hero. This connection as well as the symbolic importance of the *náqa* to the preceding journey section charge the sacrifice. In the ode of Labíd, the sacrifice marks the point at which the individual heroic boast of the poet merges with the tribal voice, the poem ending with a kind of tribal chant. In the ode of Tárafa the sacrifice goes wrong, ending with the poet's community split and his psyche split into mutually recriminating sides, one blaming, the other enraged, casting off the blame.[5] In the ode of the *suˁlúk* (brigand-poet) Shánfara, the sacrifice occurs only in a metaphor, when the brigand-poet, cut off from all community, sees himself as the hamstrung *náqa* carved up by the personifications of his many crimes. The long war of Basús, subject of many odes, was begun by the sacrilegious killing of a *náqa*. The *náqa* sacrifice is a ritual and poetic performance, sign and prediction of the precarious balance of the community and the vitality of its bonds.

Within the heroic battle-boast as an affirmation of human struggle is a meditation upon fate and the absurdity of the human condition. Two warring opponents or tribes exchange boasts and taunts. Yet within this personalized antagonism lies the suspicion that there is nothing personal at all about an encounter guided and predetermined by the hands of fate—fate as time (*dahr*) that changes and wears down all things, and fate as allotted death (*maniyya*). As the battle-boast intensifies, the hierarchies of tribal society and the sense of self-identity that the boast is upholding begin to unravel from within. The moment of death in battle unmasks the truth that the poet-hero and his enemy, kin and non-kin, self and other, father and son, can no longer be distinguished. The warrior looks into the death grin of his antagonist and sees his own reflection.

The tripartite movement of the qasida, from *nasíb* through journey to the boast, bears a remarkable resemblance to models of the quest theme in folk tale and myth. One model divides the basic mythopoetic paradigm of Western literature into three acts: an initial Edenlike condition of blissfulness that exists only as a memory; the home-leaving or expulsion of the hero and his subsequent journey; re-creation or homecoming, a return not to the original blissful lack of conflict, but to a less ideal society transformed and criticized by the culture hero's own will, act, or sacrifice.[6] This pattern, so astonishingly similar to the tripartite pattern of the qasida, was developed by an author apparently unfamiliar with pre-Islamic poetry. More recently, a close reading of several key odes has demonstrated with philological and critical precision the parallels between the qasida and the tripartite pattern of the rite of passage: initial phase of separation; a liminal phase in which the "passenger" moves beyond the margins of human community and societal restraint; and a final reaggregation into a new, more mature social role.[7]

Though the qasida is based upon an archetypal pattern with universal resonances, it achieves a distinctive mythopoetic intensity in the modulation of that pattern through its own subtle and fluid conception of the sacred. Yet perhaps the most distinctive feature of this poetry is to be found in its poetics of thematic interpermeation, the functioning of a term, epithet, image, or vignette as a matrix for associations from other, thematically distinct sections. A simple example is Shánfara's comparison of the twanging of his bow to the wailing of a grief-stricken woman. This apparently descriptive simile calls up the major *topos* of death elegy, evoking themes of community and mourning at odds with the *su'lúk* boast's explicit thematic and rhetorical intent. Within the linear and irreversible progression through the major themes of the ode, other themes, movements, and moods are evoked as subtexts, countertexts, and intertexts.

In its range of mood and mode (elegiac, lyric, bacchic, satirical, heroic, tragic, comic) and in its foundational role in subsequent literature, the qasida in Arabic civilization would be equivalent to the full variety of classical Greek literary genres subsumed into one comprehensive genre.[8] Yet it has been given less attention in the West than later, less central works, such as the *Arabian Nights* cycle. From the perspective of our "histories of civilization," rooted in the equation of civilization with the *civitas* or city, it has seemed inconceivable that a few tribes of camel-breeding bedouin, largely illiterate, largely ignored by the surrounding civilizations of Rome, Persia, and Ethiopia-Yemen, would over the space of unrecorded generations, or centuries, create one of the masterworks of world literature, a highly articulate, metrically and semantically intricate, fully achieved poetic form that was to serve as the basis for the classical Arabic language, and as a foundation of one of humankind's major civilizations. This fact left in disbelief a century of Arabist and Islamicist scholarship, a disbelief only recently giving way to appreciative wonder.[9]

A further complication is the qasida's ambivalent place within Islam. The Qur'an appropriated many of the central values of pre-Islamic poetry. The role of the *karim* (the generous one) in the qasida, for example, is reflected by its similarly central role in the Qur'an, though its heroic and poetic context has been transformed. Despite such continuities, and despite the central influence of the qasida on many areas of Islamic literature, the qasida world is in tension, a creative tension, but no less a tension, with Islam. Upon arrival at the Ka'ba, the pilgrim finds the walls hung with tapestries of rare Egyptian cloth inscribed in gold. What appears there is not poetry, however, but passages from the Qur'an.

Here are six of the odes, in full, selected with a view toward both poetic quality and balanced representation of the tradition.[10] I have not imitated the complex meter and rhyme of the original, but have used cadence, as modulated through the line breaks, to re-create the original rhythmic texture formed by the play of syntax across the meter. The goal is a rendition of the poem in a natural, idiomatic, and contemporary American verse. On the other hand, I have kept some key features, such as the relatively independent nature of each verse and the complex epithets, even where such features may be initially confusing or strange. Experiments with giving them up have proven to me their centrality. Place names carry a high semantic charge. Where their imagistic associations are striking, as in the case of the stations of the beloved's departure, I have translated them (Twin Mountain, Marblehead). Where such feature translation would be distracting or where the original feature meaning is less apparent, I have used the Arabic names (Mínan,

Rukhám, Fayd, Tilkhám). The translator walks a fine line. The new poem should not be too alien to be appreciated, but it must retain enough of the distinctive character of the original to provide a true encounter. During the ten years spent on translating these poems, I consistently found that when a verse failed to come alive in English, I had not grasped its meaning as well as I had thought—an experience that has shown me most vividly the multilayered depth and complexity of early Arabic poetry.

This is the voice of a distant, bedouin world. Yet the poetry itself has much about it that appeals to our time: sharpness of image, symbolic depth, subtlety and suppleness of allusion, honesty in encounter with the human condition, and unsentimental expression of feeling. And for all its distance from us, we encounter this poetry with a remarkable immediacy. Through the transmutations of poetry, these remembrances of the beloved, these journeys, these battles are recognized to be our own.

1. See Reynold Nicholson, *A Literary History of the Arabs* (Cambridge: Cambridge Univ. Press, 1956), pp. 101–102, and "The 'Mu'allaqāt' Problem" by Abdulla el-Tayib, an appendix to his "Pre-Islamic Poetry," *Cambridge History of Arabic Literature*, vol. 1 (Cambridge: Cambridge Univ. Press, 1983), pp. 111–113.

2. The view that the poetry is a forgery of the Islamic period has not gained much acceptance. See D. Margoliouth, "Origins of Arabic Poetry," *Journal of the Royal Asiatic Society* (1925): 417–419, where the forgery theory is propounded with abuse, typical of his time, of Arabic culture as a whole, and Taha Husayn, *Fi l adab al-jāhilī* [On Jāhilī Literature] (Cairo: Dar al-Ma'arif, n.d.).

3. See J. Monroe, "Oral Composition in Pre-Islamic Poetry," *Journal of Arabic Literature* 3 (1972): 1–53; M. Zwettler, *The Oral Tradition of Classical Arabic Poetry* (Columbus: Ohio State Univ. Press, 1978).

4. See J. Stetkevych, "Name and Epithet: The Philology and Semiotics of Animal Nomenclature in Early Arabic Poetry," *Journal of Near Eastern Studies* 45:2 (1986): 89–124; and Th. E. Homerin, "Echoes of a Thirsty Owl: Death and Afterlife in Pre-Islamic Arabic Poetry," *Journal of Near Eastern Studies* 44:3 (1985): 165–185.

5. See M. Sells, "The Mu'allaqa of Ṭarafa," *Journal of Arabic Literature* 17 (1986): 21–33. For reasons of space I have not been able to include the Mu'allaqa of Ṭarafa in this present volume.

6. Harry Slochower, *Mythopoesis: Mythic Patterns in the Literary Classics* (Detroit: Wayne State Univ. Press, 1970), pp. 22–24.

7. See S. Stetkevych, "Structuralist Interpretations of Pre-Islamic Poetry: Critique and New Directions," *Journal of Near Eastern Studies* 42:2 (1983): 85–107; "The Ṣu'lūk and His Poem: A Paradigm of Passage Manqué," *Journal of the American Oriental Society* 104.4 (1984): 661–668.

8. Whether these various movements existed as independent genres before the development of the qasida has long been a matter of speculation.

9. See J. Stetkevych, "Arabic Poetry and Assorted Poetics," *Islamic Studies: A Tradition and Its Problems* (Malibu, CA: Undena Pub., 1980), pp. 103–123; and M. Sells, "The *Qaṣīda* and the West: Self-Reflective Stereotype and Critical Encounter," *Al-ʿArabiyya* 20 (1987), pp. 307–357.

10. These six odes are only a sample of the heritage of pre-Islamic poetry. I have not included the much translated *Muʿallaqa* of Imruʾ al-Qays: see the version of Basima Bezirgan and Elizabeth Fernea in J. Berque, *Cultural Expression in Arab Society Today* (Austin: University of Texas Press, 1978). In the translations and introductions I have rendered Arabic words with an English qualitative accent, saving for the notes the more formal transliteration. The introductions are meant to serve several purposes, from introduction of key terms and conventions to critical reevaluation of the poems. Some may find it preferable to read the poem first, then the introduction, before returning to the poem. Sources include the Anbārī, Tibrīzī, and Zawzanī versions of the *Muʿallaqāt*, al-Mufaḍḍal al-Ḍabbī's *al-Mufaḍḍaliyyat*, Shantamarī's *Dīwāns of the Six Jāhilī Poets*, the Zamakhsharī, Mallūḥī, and pseudo-Mubarrad versions of Shanfarā's *Lāmiyya*, and various editions of the *dīwāns*. Technical discussion of texts and variants has been saved for another occasion.

ʿAlqama

Is What You Knew Kept Secret

This poem opens with a classic example of the remembrance of the beloved's departure, the *zaʿn*. The episode is introduced by a series of obliquely related questions concerning the beloved and the secret she entrusted to the poet. At its center is the reference to the *utrújja* (the citron, *etrog*), a word with a clearly non-Arabic origin that would have been almost as exotic to the Arabs as the Arabic word is to the modern reader. In order to preserve the intertwined associations of the rare, the sensual, and the exotic, I have kept the Arabic word in the translation. The colors of the howdah are indicated with a suggestion, somewhat shocking, of birds (probably birds of prey) confusing the rich red dye of the cloth with blood. A mention of the poet's tears, through an outrun and dissembling simile, flows into an extended depiction of the roan mare (the *náqa*) pulling an irrigation bag, with all the associations of fertility and overflowing abundance that the memory of the beloved evokes. A final, proclaimed effort to renounce memory of Sálma is followed by the most specific memory of her, of the folds and clings of her garment. This is the closest the poem comes to describing her, her features still, as always, poetically veiled.

The journey begins with the night courser, *náqa*, only to turn rather quickly to a one-verse mention of the "tuck-bellied brindle-leg" (bull oryx), a mention that is as compelling as it is brief, as if the image were glimpsed in the depths of the imagination. The substitutions end with the "red-legged clump-wing" (ostrich), at which point the poem opens onto a classic tableau: the male ostrich browsing, then racing back to the nest (here, as if in two temporally separate flashes, racing back once to the eggs, another time to the chicks), the thin mouth, feet flying past the small, earless head, a clucking that is like the babble of foreigners. The babbling foreigners are Byzantine Romans (*rum*), a reversal of the etymology of the English term *barbarism* as the babble of those speaking other (non-Greek) tongues. Here it is the Greeks who are the babblers to a bedouin poet at home in a highly articulate cultural-linguistic world of his own. The comparison of the wing carriage of the ostrich to a tent shows how such standard features, fine-honed over generations and selected down to the precise simile, can achieve the most striking originality in how they are performed. In the Muʿállaqa of ʿAntara, the same

11

comparison is made, with a subtle and important difference. ʿAlqama's comparison fits in perfectly with the erotic and humorous mood of the entire ostrich scene, the wing carriage compared to a "caved-in heap of a tent set up wrong by a clumsy maid." In ʿAntara, the ostrich performance is dominated by a more tragic mood, as is the ode as a whole, the wing carriage compared to a "funeral litter above a tented bier."

The boast is introduced by a powerful set of proverbs. Proverbs most often appear in the qasida individually, usually in the second hemistich of a verse, offering a timeless perspective in balance with the particular situation evoked in the first hemistich, as in a verse that occurs later in the poem: "Whatever the stakes, the loser pays." At times proverbs dominate an ode, as in the Muʿállaqa of Zuháyr. Here they extend to seven verses, carefully balanced with the other sections of the poem. At any point in the qasida, the proverbial meditation on fate and loss can be evoked in a variety of ways with the subtlest movement in grammar or diction.

The wine song, one of the earliest in a long line of homages to the magic qualities of wine, presents the wine with a ritual formality. This banquet is followed by the image of the warrior on horseback, enduring hunger, heat, and sandstorms. The ode also ends with pageantry, as the horse and camel are led in a procession with praise of their qualities and lineage. Pageantry ties together several movements: the *nasíb* scene of the maiden servants leading in the howdah camels (which are always stallions); the veiling of the beloved within her howdah drapery and the procession that leads her away from the poet; the bringing out and unveiling of the wine; and the formal procession of horse and camel mare that closes the poem. The reference to the camels pleading like a tambourine being torn on the heights carries a special force due to its echoing of similar comparisons, usually to mourning women wailing on a high ridge.

This ode of ʿAlqama is a balanced representation of the qasida model at what seems to be a very early period. It is vivid in its imagistic surface, and unsentimental in its hesitancy to reveal directly the interior world of emotion, allowing the material image or impersonal proverb in almost every case to speak, articulating its secret within the subtle resonances of a formal pageantry and its brilliant poetic veils.

ʿAlqama ibn ʿAbada of the tribe of Tamīm is said to have lived in the sixth century C.E., to have been a poetic rival of Imruʾ al-Qays, and to have been involved in the struggle between the Arab kingdoms of Ghassān (a satellite of the Byzantine empire) and Lakhm (a satellite of the Persian empire).

The meter is quantitative (a long vowel, diphthong, or vowel followed by a double consonant forming a long foot, all other vowels forming a short foot). The meter is the *basīṭ*, based upon the feet: ˘ (or –) – ˘ –/– (or ˘) ˘ –. The first verse would be scanned as follows, a macron indicating a naturally long vowel:

$$\text{–} \quad \text{–} \; \text{˘} \; \text{–} \; / \text{˘} \; \text{˘} \; \text{–} / \text{–} \; \text{–} \; \text{˘} \; \text{–} / \text{–} \; \text{–}$$

hal mā ʿalimta wa mā stūdiʿta maktūmū

$$\text{–} \quad \text{–} \; \text{˘} \; \text{–}/\text{–} \quad \text{˘} \; \text{–} / \text{–} \quad \text{–} \; \text{˘} \; \text{–} / \text{–} \; \text{–}$$

am ḥabluhā idh naʾatka l-yawma maṣrūmū

Translator's divisions: *nasīb*; journey, with *nāqa* ("night courser"), oryx bull ("tuck-bellied brindle-leg"), and ostrich ("red-legged clump-wing"); proverbs; wine song; horse scene and pageantry.

Is What You Knew Kept Secret

Is what you came to know,
   given in trust,
kept secret? Is her bond to you
   broken, now that she is far?

        Does a grown man weeping
        tears without end for those he loved,
           the dawn of parting,
        receive his fair reward?

By the time I knew,
   they had set their leave,
all the camel stallions
   standing bridled before dawn,

        Camel stallions of her tribe
        led in by maiden servants,
           then loaded,
        bundles bound in Tazídi brocade,

While birds hung in the air
   plucking at dye streaks and tassels
as if they'd been stained
   heartsblood crimson.

        They carried an *utrújja* away.
        A saffron-scented perfume trailed.
        Before the senses even now
        her fragrance lingers,

The folds of her hair
   redolent as musk when the pod is opened.
Reaching out to touch it
   even the stuff-nosed is overcome.

        Liken my weeping eye to a water bag
        dragged down the well slope
           by a roan mare, withers
        bound to the saddle-stay,

For a full season unsaddled,
   until her hump hardened,
firm as the rounded side
   of a smith's bellows,

Cured of the mange
and covered
with a resinous balm,
clear and pure,

Spilling water into channels
as grain husks part
from the ripening fruit,
the flooded slopes flowing over.

To remember Sálma! to recall
times spent with her
is folly, conjecture about the other side,
a casting of stones,

Breast sash crossed
and falling, gown folds
at the hip, clinging, tender
as a gazelle fawn reared within the yard.

———————

Will I overtake
her far-flung tribe's rear guard
on a night courser,
solid as a worn boulder in a stream,

Dromedarian lips,
tinged by a wash of green mallow
that foams up
over cheek and jaw?

On one like that,
borne through the desert,
ranging far, while in the shadows
the owl sends forth a muffled cry.

She side-eyes the whip,
silent as a tuck-bellied brindle-leg,
ears sharpened
to the softest sound,

Or like a red-legged clump-wing,
bitterapple and castorberry
ripening for him
behind the twisting dune.

At the black-banded colocynth
   he lingers,
cracking pods,
   and snipping sprouts of grey castor,

        Mouth like the split in a stick—
      you barely make it out—
        and ears, tufted markings,
      as if he'd been docked,

Until he remembers some eggs,
   disquieted by a day
of drizzle and wind
   and a covering of cloud.

        He quickens his pace,
      without strain,
        whisking along just short of all out,
      untiring,

Split-foot flying
   past his bulging eye,
as if he were wary of ill luck,
   fear-quickened,

        A strider, forechest
      like the string of a lyre,
        like a water bird
      in a meadow pool.

He doubles back to a down-cropped
   brood of nestlings
that appear when they tumble over
   like a clod-covered root,

        Circling the nest hollow,
      circling again,
        searching for tracks . . .

Until he reaches
   as the sun's horn rises
the nest hollow
   and a heap of eggs,

Beckoning to them
with a cackling and clucking
like the babble of Greeks
in their fortresses,

Small-headed, thin-necked,
wings and chest
like a caved-in heap of a tent
set up wrong by a clumsy maid.

A female draws near,
long neck lowered,
responding
with a warbling cry.

Every tribe,
though great, though many,
will one day see its chief
struck down by the hearthstones of evil.

Praise can't be purchased
except for a price
men begrudge,
one that is well known.

Generosity is a blight on riches,
an abode of loss.
What you hoard is left over,
the object of scorn.

What you own
is a wooly plaything,
growing long on stubby sheep,
then shorn.

He who gains his quarry
the day of the raid
finds it wherever he turns.
He who misses, misses out.

Hot-neck folly will cross your path.
You don't have to track it down.
Foresight and self-command
make themselves scarce in the crowd.

Whoever comes upon crows
   and scatters them for an omen
though secure at the time
   is fated to ruin.

      Every fortress,
      long safe on great pillars,
      will one day
      be razed to the ground.

I could well see the drinkers,
   among them a ringing lyre,
men laid low
   by golden, foaming wine,

      The drink of a potentate,
      aged by tavernkeepers
        for a special occasion.
      It'll take you up and spin you around.

For the headache it's a cure.
   A jolt of it won't harm you.
No dizziness from it
   will mix in your brain,

      A vintage of 'Anah, a slammer,
      for a full year unexposed,
        kept in a clay-stoppered jug
      with a waxen seal,

Glistening in its decanter,
   while a foreign-born page,
mouth covered with a cotton band,
   pours it,

      Flagon like a gazelle
      high on the cliff face,
        neck and spout sealed
      with a linen sieve.

Its keeper brings it out into the sun.
   It flashes white,
ringed by branches of sweet basil,
   fragrance brimming over.

Many times have I set out early
against a peer,
accompanied by a firm,
fine-honed, piercing blade.

Many times have I gambled,
trusting hunger to an arrow
carved from hard wood,
bound with sinew and notched.

They put their stallions up for wager.
I offered mine first.
Whatever the stakes,
the loser pays.

I might well ride with a band of braves,
no provisions
but a food sack green with mold
and some stinking meat.

Many times have I mounted the saddle frame,
face seared
by a day of the Gemini
and pestilent, blistering winds,

Burning,
as if one were cloaked
and turbaned, wrap on wrap
in the kindled air.

I might well lead before the tribe
a tall mare,
as if her lineage, known to all,
were leading her,

With a flawless splint bone
and a flawless pastern,
with hoof walls
trimmed and intact,

With shanks like the base of a palm branch,
legs like a Náhdi's staff,
feet with a hoof frog as tough
as a hard-gnawed date pit from Qúrran,

She follows a troop of black dromedaries
    that cry out when driven
like a tambourine
    torn on the heights.

        On one side a spring-born calf
      is pleading, while on the other
         the old camels, humps high,
      bellow,

Led by a stallion,
    worn and tried,
an old-timer,
    meaty, huge.

Shánfara

Arabian Ode in "L"

The "Arabian Ode [Rhyming] in 'L'" (*Lámiyyat al-ʿArab*) is the most famous *suʿlúk* qasida. It appears to neglect the normal qasida tripartite pattern, and, like the *suʿlúk* or brigand himself, to wander without apparent sense of progression or goal. The poem begins with Shánfara abandoned by, or abandoning, his tribe, claiming that he has better friends in the desert scavengers and in his sword, heart, and bow. In embracing this paradoxical community of marauding animals, weapons, and self, Shánfara refers to himself as a *karím*. The term is often translated as "generous one" or "noble," but its range of heroic values is so comprehensive that I have rendered it as "man," allowing the poem to fill in its meaning. The *Lámiyya* has become a touchstone for the ethos of the pre-Islamic *karím*, even though on the formal level the *suʿlúk* inverts many of the *karím*'s most important traits.

The poem then turns to abusive satire (*hijá*). The traits ridiculed (vanity, laziness, inability to follow through on plans, susceptibility to being flustered or taken unawares) are associated with *jahl*, an undisciplined impetuosity opposed to the virtue of *hilm* (self-command, calm and seasoned calculation of one's situation). This poem is a vivid manifestation of the heroic *hilm-jahl* ethos before its transformation by the Qurʾan into a religious ethic.

The satirical tone grows suddenly somber as the desert overcomes the unskilled traveler, "lagging, frantic, losing his way." Two similes then lead into extended animal vignettes. In each case the initial descriptive point (patient as a wolf, swift as a sand grouse) is both accomplished and outrun as the poetic voice overflows into two of the more famous extended similes in Arabic poetry.

The voice then becomes more personal. In a passage of psychological intensity, Shánfara personifies his crimes as drawing lots for his "hamstrung flesh." The heroic boast is being inverted. In the standard boast, the hero reaffirms his role as a *karím* by sacrificing his *náqa* and distributing the meat through the *máysir* game. In Shánfara's metaphor, it is the poet himself who is depicted as the slaughtered *náqa*. This portrayal of the *suʿlúk* as his own riding camel echoes a similar inversion earlier in the poem where the poet refers to his "sole pads." The paradox within the outcast's assertion of the quintessentially tribal role of the *karím* is most evident here where the camel sacrifice and the *máysir* reference (starving wolves as thin as arrow shafts rattling around in the hand of a gambler) come to symbolize not the plenty of the tribal benefactor, but bare-boned privation.

After burning his bow and arrow wood (another loss of cultural identity) on a night of ill luck, Shánfara haunts the fringes of community, preying upon it through a night raid that is presented with a chilling indirection ("and a man, no, men don't act like that"). The reference to a jinni may recall the "mother of dust," mentioned just before the raid and which may be an allusion to the *ghul*, that female jinni known to change forms constantly, bewilder the traveler, and lead him to destruction. After a final journey scene, again with the hero traveling on foot, *su'lúk* style, the ode ends with a moment of quiet lyricism, the poet standing unnoticed amid the mountain goats, as if he himself were a mountain goat or mountain antelope ("white-foot," "tall-horned").

In this *su'lúk* ode there is no remembrance of the beloved. Shánfara's rejoicing in the departure of his tribe at the beginning of the poem is an ironic countertype to the lament over the beloved's departure. What boast elements there are, such as the camel sacrifice, are also inverted. Even the journey, the major theme of this poem, is given an ironic performance. Shánfara travels on foot rather than by camel mare, never reaching a goal of reintegration with society, but—like his starving wolves—is passed endlessly on from one desert into another.

Still, what is formally absent is brought back in subtle ways. The lyrical ending of the poem recalls the idyllic animal poses of the *nasíb*, a resonance compounded by the allusion, brought in through a dissembled simile, to women draped in flowing shawls. The perpetual solitude of the antisocial *su'lúk* is countered by the images of community that appear in his similes ("like droves of camels at a wayside pool"). Especially powerful are the resonances of the dirge, a *topos* that often formed a separate poem of its own and which was closely related to the *nasíb*: the dirge being a lament for the deceased loved one, the *nasíb* a lament for the absent beloved. Images of mourning women recur throughout the poem. Within the twanging of the bow and behind the howling of the wolves, one hears the echo of dirge, and through its associations, the lament for the lost beloved, the lost garden, the broken community, echoes of a sadness particularly haunting in its partial concealment beneath the *su'lúk* demeanor that "keeps its composure over what it hides."

The legend of Shanfarā of the tribe of Azd is particularly complex. He is said to have been captured from his natal tribe by a clan of the Fahm, then sold back to an Azdite clan, the Banū Salāmān, in exchange for a captive member of the Fahm. When his natal tribe treated him as a foreigner, he swore revenge, joined up with the Fahm, and spent his life as a *ṣuʿlūk*, raiding the Salāmān. He avenged the murder of his adoptive father (according to another version, his natal father) by killing a man during a sacred pilgrimage and just before his death he is said to have recited the famous verses asking that his body be left unburied for the hyenas. The historical accuracy of the legend and of the *Lāmiyya*'s attribution to Shanfarā are in doubt. (Even in medieval times it was considered by some to be the work of the Basran grammarian of the Islamic period, Khalaf al-Aḥmar.) The legend has been shown to be a reflection of central themes within the *Lāmiyya* and *ṣuʿlūk* poetry generally: confusion of kinship and identity; inversion of tribal values concerning the pilgrimage, rules of war, and the burial of the dead; and inversion of blood vengeance as an act to be carried out, by definition, against non-kin. See S. Stetkevych, "Archetype and Attribution in Early Arabic Poetry: Al-Shanfarā and the *Lāmiyyat al-ʿArab*," *International Journal of Middle East Studies* 18 (1986): 361–90.

Verses 8–9, generally considered problematical, have been omitted.

The meter is the *ṭawīl*, the most common of the pre-Islamic meters, based upon the feet: ˘ – ˘ (or –) / ˘ – ˘ (or –) –.

˘ – – / ˘ – ˘ ˘ – – / ˘ – – ˘ / ˘ – – ˘ –
aqīmū banī ummī ṣudūra matiyyikum

˘ – – / ˘ – – – / ˘ – – / ˘ – ˘ –
fa innī ilā qawmin siwākum la amyalū

Translator's divisions: the break with the tribe; *hijāʾ* and *ṣuʿlūk* boast; the wolf scene; the sand grouse; tracked down by his crimes; raid, *ṣuʿlūk* journey, and ending.

Arabian Ode in "L"

Get up the chests of your camels
    and leave, sons
of my mother. I lean to a tribe
    other than you.

        What must be is at hand.
        The moon is full,
          · mounts and saddle frames secured
        for distant crossings.

In this land is a refuge for a man
    from wrongs,
for one fearing scalding hatred,
    a place to withdraw.

        By your life! It crowds on no man
       who travels by night,
          in fear or in desire,
        and keeps his wits about him.

I have in place of you other kin:
    the wolf, unwearying runner,
the darting sand leopard,
    the bristle-necked hyena.

        These are my clan. They don't reveal
    a secret given in trust,
          and they don't abandon a man
        for his crimes.

They are the scornful ones,
    the fierce, though I
at first sight of the prey
    am fiercer.

        As recompense for losing those
    who don't repay a favor,
          in whose nearness
        I cannot feel ease,

I have three friends: a brave
    heart, a bare
blade, and a long
    bow of yellow wood,

Smooth and taut,
sonorous,
bedecked with jeweled tokens,
secured with a crossbelt,
And when it lets the arrow slip
it twangs,
like a child-bereft mother,
grief-struck, who moans and wails.

———————

I'm no quick-to-thirst,
herd ill-pastured at dusk,
calves ill-fed
though their mother's udders are untied,
No foul-breathed cringer,
wife-clinging,
asking her in every affair
what to do,
No ostrich,
gangly, stupefied,
as if a sparrow were beating up and down
in his heart,
No malingerer, stay-at-home,
woman-chaser,
evening and morning coated with kohl
and perfume,
No tick,
worthless, indolent,
leaping up, when startled,
unarmed,
Nor bewildered by the dark
when the towering emptiness
turns astray the traveler, lagging,
frantic, losing his way.
When my sole pads
meet the gravel flint
it flies up sparking,
shattered.

I push hunger on
   until it dies,
drive attention from it,
   forget.

            I'd sooner slurp the dust,
         a dry mouthful,
            than take some man's
         condescending favors.

Were I not shunning blame
   I would lack
no food, no drink,
   no ease of life,

            But this hard soul
         gives me no rest
            when wronged
         until I move on,

Wrapping my insides
   around an empty stomach pit,
like a weaver's threads
   spun and twisted.

            _____

            I part at dawn on meager fare
         like a wolf
            led on, desert into desert,
         scrawny, grey.

He sets out at dawn, hungry,
   quick into the wind,
slicing down where the ravine ends
   and veering.

            He moves on in pursuit of food.
            It eludes him.
            He howls. His mates respond,
            hunger-worn,

Thin as the new moon,
   ashen-faced, like arrow shafts
rattling around
   in the hand of a gambler,

Like a queen bee,
swarm roused
by the two poles of a cliff-dangling
honey-gatherer,

Wide-jawed, gape-mouthed,
as if their jaws
were the sides of a split stick,
grinning, grim.

He howls in the empty spaces,
they howl,
as if they and he were bereaved women
on the high ridge, wailing.

His eyelids sag. He grows silent.
They follow his lead.
They, he, forlorn,
take heart from one another.

He turns back. They turn back,
surging, hard pressed,
keeping composure
over what they hide.

———————

The sand grouse drink what I leave behind.
They approach the water hole
after a night journey,
their sides rumbling.

I resolved. They did.
We raced. Their wings fell limp
while I stood in front at ease
with my robe tucked up.

I turned away.
They tumbled to the rim,
crops and gullets
squeezing and pulsing,

As if their clatter
on both sides of the water hole
were groups of men from caravans,
letting themselves down,

Congregating from all sides
    and taken in
like droves of camels
    at a wayside pool.

        They gulped swiftly and passed on
        at dawn
            like panic-stricken riders
        from Uháza.

I know the earth's face well.
    There I stretch out,
restless,
    dried out vertebrae and a crooked back,

        An arm for a pillow,
        worn to the bone,
            joints standing up like bone cubes
        strewn by a gambler.

And if the mother of dust
    grieves for Shánfara now,
long did she find satisfaction in him
    before!

            His crimes track him down.
            They cast lots
                for the choicest piece
            of his hamstrung flesh.

When he sleeps
    they spend the night,
eyes open, quick to his ruin,
    working their way in.

            Shánfara, friend of cares!
            Time after time they return
                like quartan fever
            or worse.

When they come down
    I drive them out.
They turn back from all sides
    upon me.

Though you might see me
sun-beaten as a sand daughter,
ragged, shoeless,
with worn feet,

Still am I the master of patience,
wearing its armor
over the heart of a sand cat,
shod with resolution.

Sometimes I have nothing,
sometimes all I need.
Only one who gives himself,
far-seeing, will prosper.

I don't lose nerve in adversity,
exposing weakness,
nor do I prance, self-satisfied,
in my riches.

The hot-neck fool will not provoke
my self-command, and I am not seen
begging at the heels of conversations
and slandering.

On how many a night of ill luck
when the hunter burns his bow
for fuel,
and his arrow wood.

Have I trodden through darkness and drizzle,
on fire with hunger,
grinding inside, shivering,
filled with dread.

Then have I widowed women
and orphaned children,
returning as I began,
the night a blacker black.

When next morning in Ghumaysá
two groups met,
one asking about me,
the other being asked:

29

"Last night our dogs were whining."

        "A wolf prowling, or a hyena?"

"Just a faint sound, then silence."

        "Perhaps a startled grouse, or a hawk?"

"If a jinni,
    what an ill-boding night visitor!
and a man, no,
    men don't act like that."

        To how many a day of the dog star,
        when the sun drools heat
        and snakes writhe
        on the burning ground,

Have I turned my face,
    no veil to protect it
but the tattered shreds
    of an Athami cloak,

        With hair down my back,
        flying up
        when the wind takes it
        in uncombed clumps,

Unoiled, unloused,
    encrusted,
a full turn of seasons
    without a rinse of mallow.

        How many a desert plain, wind-swept,
        like the surface of a shield,
        empty, impenetrable,
        have I cut through on foot,

Joining the near end to the far,
    then looking out from a summit,
crouching sometimes,
    then standing,

While mountain goats, flint-yellow,
graze around me,
    meandering like maidens
draped in flowing shawls.

They become still in the setting sun,
    around me, as if I were a white-foot,
bound for the high mountain meadow,
    tall-horned.

Labíd

The Mu^cállaqa

In this poem the traces of the beloved's campsite reappear in differing forms: torrent beds that are highlighted as they are worn away; writings and inscriptions effaced and then restored; a tattoo, symbol of the unchanging, that fades and is renewed; the ruins of Nawár's campsite and the scene, remembered or imagined, that they conjure. The line between remembrance and imagination at this point is difficult to find. The spring rains, flowering meadows, and tranquil poses of desert animals such as the gazelle, ostrich, and "wide-of-eyes" (oryx doe) are evoked through remembrance of the beloved, Nawár. The underlying archetype—beloved as lost garden—begins to unfold. The interplay of absence and presence, effacement and manifestation, barrenness and verdant meadows, ends in a final contrast between silence and speech. Although renewed, the inscriptions are indecipherable. When the poet questions the ruins, they are *summ* (hard, deaf), offering only a lapidary silence, or words whose meaning is unclear.

After the departure of the howdah caravan (*za^cn*) a more distant perspective is offered, the group fading into the distance like "tamarisks and boulders on the slopes of Bíshah." The precise and specific delineation of the monuments that Nawár passes almost masks the fact that the poet is not with her and can only imagine the trajectory of her journey. When the tension between this geographical and temporal distancing, on the one hand, and the poetic and imaginative lingering over her presence, on the other, reaches the breaking point, the journey section abruptly begins: "Cut the bond . . . ."

In the journey, the *náqa* ("journey-worn mare") is displaced first by the episode of the onagers ("sheen-of-udder" and "white-belly"), displaced in turn by the episode of the "wild one" or "flat-nosed one" (the oryx doe) who loses her fawn to wolves, is cornered by hunters, and kills two hunting dogs (Kasábi—literally Fetch—and Sukhám). An associative polarity is generated: highlands, drought, heat, mating, and endurance in the onager section, lowlands, flooding, death of offspring, and fragility in the oryx section. By the time we reach the oryx, the initial "likeness" of the *náqa* has turned to polarity, the associations of the oryx in almost direct contrast with the quasi-elemental endurance of the *náqa*. A different kind of valence-reversal occurs between the oryx in the journey and the oryx in the *nasíb*. In the *nasíb*, the water was associated with idyll, the oryx ("wide-of-eyes") was presented in an Edenlike domesticity, and human presence or company (*uns*) was the object of yearning. In the oryx scene of the journey, water is associated with flooding, loss, and death, the oryx ("wild one") with a more vulnerable and more sensual world, and human presence with dread.

The boast is ushered in by Labíd's famous wine song, the poet protesting all too much how well he has forgotten Nawár. The wine song is followed by a brief, but powerful depiction of the hero on horseback descending a mountain: "The sun's hand dropped into thickening darkness. . . ." The vantage-point scene, with the way-marks and terrain obscured in dust, recalls the reference to a vantage point in the onager tableau of the journey ("the way-stones charged with fear"), while contrasting with the topographical clarity of the stages of Nawár's journey recounted by a poet who was not there.

The culmination of the boast is the ritual slaughter of the *náqa*, and the division of the meat through the *máysir* game. At this moment the individual voice of the poet is subsumed into the collective voice of the tribe, and the various currents of the ode, deep, wandering, diffuse, come together in a final torrent of tribal chant. What is chanted is the *sunna* (path, custom) of the ancestors, and the *shar'* (division, sharing) of the tribe. Special insistence is given to the feeding and sheltering of those with weak kinship bonds. The destitute are likened to a *balíyya* or ghost mare, the riding mare that was tethered to the tomb of her fallen master and left to die. This haunting image highlights the symbolic association between the *náqa* and the self of the poet-hero and charges the *náqa* sacrifice with that association.

A later reference to the house with high roofs, and to the lord of that house, carries a charged religious sense, a sense reflected in early Islamic uses of the term "house" (*bayt*). The entire section may be a response to the Qur'anic criticism of pre-Islamic Arabian society for neglecting the orphan and the needy and to the prophetic *súnna* and *shar'* offered in place of that of the tribes. According to Labíd's legend, the poet lived to a Methuselan age, and died some forty years after the founding of Islam in 622 C.E. The appearance at the end of this poem of the central pre-Islamic ritual of camel sacrifice in what appears to be a response to Qur'anic criticism, gives the poem the aura of a final assertion of the tribal ethos in the face of the prophetic challenge.

Labíd ibn Rabí'a of the tribe of 'Amr is said to have lived to an age of 150, championed his tribe before the court at al-Ḥíra, accepted Islam, and renounced poetry under the caliph 'Umar.

The meter is the *kāmil*, in which the basic pattern, repeated three times per hemistich, is: – (or ˘ ˘) – ˘ –. The rhyme (*hā*) results in a distinctive feature of the poem. The syllable *hā* is often the feminine or plural personal pronoun, but it is often used in this poem in a vague referential sense, setting up an interesting, nonpersonal sense of "its."

˘ ˘ — ˘ —/˘ ˘ — ˘ — / ˘ ˘ — ˘ —
ʿafat id-diyāru maḥalluhā fa muqāmuhā

˘ ˘ — ˘ —/˘ ˘ — ˘ — / ˘ ˘ — ˘ —
bi minan taʾabbada ghawluhā fa rijāmuhā

Translator's divisions: *nasīb*; *nāqa* ("journey-worn mare") and onagers ("the sheen-of-udder" and the "white-belly"); the oryx doe ("wild one," "flat-nosed one"); wine song; boast, with horseback vignette, *nāqa* sacrifice, and tribal boast.

The Mu'állaqa

The tent marks in Mínan are worn away,
  where she encamped
and where she alighted,
    Ghawl and Rijám left to the wild,

        And the torrent beds of Rayyán
        naked tracings,
          worn thin, like inscriptions
        carved in flattened stones,

Dung-stained ground
  that tells the years passed
since human presence, months of peace
  gone by, and months of war,

        Replenished by the rain stars
        of spring, and struck
          by thunderclap downpour, or steady,
        fine-dropped, silken rains,

From every kind of cloud
  passing at night,
darkening the morning,
  or rumbling in peals across the evening sky.

        The white pondcress has shot upward,
        and on the wadi slopes,
          gazelles among their newborn,
        and ostriches,

And the wide-of-eyes,
  silent above monthling fawns.
On the open terrain
  yearlings cluster.

        The rills and the runlets
        uncovered marks like the script
          of faded scrolls
        restored with pens of reed,

Or tracings of a tattoo woman:
  beneath the indigo powder,
sifted in spirals,
    the form begins to reappear.

35

I stopped to question them.
How is one to question
    deaf, immutable,
    inarticulate stones?

Stripped bare now,
    what once held all that tribe—
they left in the early morning
    leaving a trench and some thatch,

                They stirred longing in you
            as they packed up their howdahs,
                    disappearing in the lairs of cotton,
                frames creaking,

Post-beams covered
    with twin-rodded curtains
of every kind of cloth brocade
    and a black, transparent, inner veil,

                Strung out along the route
            in groups, like oryx does of Túdih,
                or Wájran gazelles, white fawns
            below them, soft necks turning,

They faded into the distance
    appearing in the shimmering haze
like tamarisks and boulders
    on the slopes of Bíshah.

                But why recall Nawár?
            She's gone.
                Her ties and bonds to you
            are broken.

The Múrrite lady
    has lodged in Fayd,
then joined up with the Hijázi clans.
    Who are you to aspire to reach her,

                On the eastern slopes
            of Twin Mountains or Muhájjar?
                Lonebutte has taken her in,
            then Marblehead,

Then Tinderlands
    if she heads toward Yemen—
I imagine her there—or at Thrall Mountain
    or in the valley of Tilkhám.

        Cut the bond
        with one you cannot reach!
        The best of those who make a bond
        are those who can break it.

Give to one who seems to care,
    give again,
but if the love goes lame and stumbles,
    you can break it off

            On a journey-worn mare,
            worn to a remnant,
                with sunken loins
                and a sunken hump.

When flesh shrinks back
    around the joints,
and at the limits of weariness
    ankle thongs fray,

            She is as fleet in the bridle
            as a reddish cloud
                emptied of water
                skimming along on the south wind.

Or a sheen-of-udder,
    mate of a rutted white-belly.
Gnashing and kicking, the driving off of rivals,
    has turned him sallow.

            Bite-scarred, wary,
            he takes her high
                into the hill curves, pregnant,
                recalcitrant, craving.

Above the craglands of Thalabút
    he climbs the vantage points,
wind-swept,
    the way-stones charged with fear,

Until they scrape back through
the six dry months of Jumáda,
month on month of thirst,
surviving on dew.

They bring their course
to a binding plan—
strength of intent
is in the twist of the strands.

Pasterns tear in the briar grass.
Summer winds
flare into dust squalls
and burning winds of Sumúm.

They contend in raising dust.
Its shadow soars
like the smoke of a firebrand,
kindling set ablaze,

Fanned by the north wind,
stoked with brushweed,
the smoke of a blazing,
high-billowing fire.

He pushes on,
keeping her ahead.
She balks.
He drives her forward

Until they break
into the midst of a stream,
split the brimming flow
and clustered reeds,

An enclosing stand of rushes,
some trampled,
some standing,
hedging them in with shade.

Or was it a wild one,
wolf-struck?
She lagged behind the herd.
Its lead animal had been her stay.

A flat-nosed one who lost her young,
    she does not cease
circling the dune slopes
    and lowing,

            For a white fawn, rolled in the dust
            and dismembered
                by contending wolves, ashen,
            not about to give up their portion.

They chanced upon her
    while she was unaware
and struck. The arrows of fate
    do not miss their prey.

            She passes the night
            in continuous curtains of rain
                washing around the dune tufts
            in a steady stream,

Flowing along the line of her back,
    runlet on runlet,
on a night the stars
    are veiled in cloud.

            She enters a gnarled tangle
            of roots, casting about
                with her horns, at the base of the dune
            as it drifts and falls away,

Glowing in the face
    of the dark, luminous,
like a seaman's pearl
    come unstrung.

            As night parts from dawn
            she appears in the early light,
                leg shafts slipping
            on the hard, wet sand,

Splashing, confused,
    through the pools of Suʿáʾid,
back and forth,
    seven pairs of nights and days,

Until, hope gone,
    her once-full udder dries,
        though suckling and weaning
    are not what withered it down.

She makes out the sound of men,
    muffled, striking fear
from the hidden side,
    human presence, her affliction.

        Dawn finds her turning,
    front and rear,
        placing behind her and ahead
    the source of fear,

Until the archers give up
    and send in their well-trained,
lop-eared, rawhide-collared
    hunting hounds.

        They run her down.
    She wheels upon them
        with a horn, point and shaft,
    like a Samharíyya spear,

Driving them off,
    sensing death upon her
if she fails, certain,
    fated, near.

        Kasábi bears down on her.
    He is smeared in blood,
        and Sukhám, in his place of attack,
    is left to die.

_____

On one like that,
    when shimmerings dance
in the forenoon
    and hills are gowned in mirage,

        I bring the issue to a close,
    not held back by doubt
        or by some critic's rummaging around
    for something there to blame.

Or didn't you know, Nawár,
   that I
am one who ties a love knot
   and cuts it free?

         Who abandons a place
         that no longer pleases,
            unless ill fate cleave
         to that some certain self of mine.

You don't know, no,
   how many nights,
bright-faced, with drinking company
   and delicious entertainment

            I have spent in talk! Showing up
            at the innkeeper's banner
               at the moment it is raised,
            when the wine is choice,

Paying any price for every vintage
   aged in blackened skins
and tar-smeared jugs,
   seals broken,

            For a pure morning draught
            and the play of a singing girl
               upon her lute, fingers slipping
            softly across the strings,

Rising early to outstrip
   the rooster's morning call
for a second round that quenches
   when sleepers just begin to stir.

            ──────────

            On how many a cold and windy morning
            have I held steady
               as the reins fall
            into the hands of the north wind,

Tribe-defender,
   sword on a fiery steed,
my cross-sash her bridle,
   riding out at dawn

41

To climb to a vantage point
over a close-walled gorge
hidden in dust,
dust covering the way-marks.

The sun's hand dropped
into thickening darkness,
the mouths of the ridge passage
concealed in veils of shadow.

I descended to the plain,
mare standing like a palm,
smooth, towering trunk
thwarting the date cutters.

I drove her on to the pace of an ostrich
and faster,
until she grew hot
and her bones softened,

Saddle sliding
as her neck poured sweat,
girth strap drenched
in hot foam.

Head raised, she stretched
in the bridle, and veered
like a water-bound pigeon
when the flock surges.

How many strangers
in how many an unruly mob
where gains are sought,
blame feared,

Lion-necked, threat-spewing,
demanding blood,
as if they were desert jinn,
feet anchored in stone,

Have I given the lie
in what they claimed,
affirming my share of right,
lorded over by no prince of theirs.

How many times have I called
    for a *máysir* slaughter
and the gaming lots
    of notched arrow shafts,

        Calling the throw
            for a calfless or nursing mare,
        the portions parceled out
            to all the client clans,

Distant clients and guests
    as if they'd come down
to Tabála
    where valleys are green,

        Seeking refuge among the tent ropes,
        weary as a stumbling camel,
            weary as a ghost mare,
        white-humped, left to die.

They show up when the winds wail,
    the weak of kin,
the broken kin, the orphaned,
    to be given an equal's share.

        There is yet among us
        when the council meets,
            one who seizes the moment,
        who takes on the burden,

Who divides and assigns,
    who raises high the rights of some,
others,
    driving into the ground,

        As he deems fit, magnanimous,
        munificent,
            gracious,
        seeking plunder and gaining it.

From a clan whose fathers
    have shown the way.
For every warrior band
    there is a guide and a way.

Their honor untarnished,
their action never fallow,
their judgment does not lean
with the winds of desire.

When trust was portioned out
among the tribe,
the divider bestowed on us
the greater share.

Be content with what the sire
has given.
He who portioned merit out among us
is most knowing.

He built for us a house
with lofty roof.
Boys and full-aged men
ascend to it.

They are the protectors
when the tribe is pressed,
they are the riders,
they are the rulers.

They are life-spring
to dependents among them,
to those without provider,
when the year grows long.

They are the tribe
when the envier drags his foot
and the vile one
leans to the enemy.

ʿAntara

The Muʿállaqa

"O abode of ʿAbla in al-Jiwáʾi, speak!" The invocation becomes incantatory with the repetition of the phrase *dára ʿábla* (abode of ʿAbla). In this, the most tragic of the odes, the erotic or life-affirming element of speech, as reflected in the remembrance of the beloved and the wine song, sounds with consummate beauty, only to lose itself in the chaos of self-perpetuating, reciprocal violence.

In the first ten verses, reference to the beloved oscillates between the second and third person, and she is addressed by several names and nicknames (ʿAbla, Bint Mákhrami, Umm al-Háytham). The grammatical and referential instability surrounds a blunt statement of separation: "killing her kinsmen, coveting, by your father's life, what is not to be." The social context—beloved's tribe and poet's tribe at war with one another—will gradually open onto a similarly tragic psychic state, as differences between self and other, kin and non-kin, warrior and enemy, break down. Mention of the wet mouth of the beloved then leads to a series of outrun similes: mouth to perfume, to garden, to rains, ending in a particularly beautiful garden scene, with a fly, alone, buzzing like a wine drinker humming a tune, or a one armed man bent over the flint. Only the last simile, so perfectly apt, prefigures the theme of mutilation that will gradually dominate the poem.

The journey is foreshadowed by the poet-hero on horseback, a motif that before the boast is always brief, often (as here and in the ode of Dhu al-Rúmma) introduced by the thought of the beloved's evening and dawn travels. The poem then moves into the *náqa* performance, in which is embedded an extended simile involving the ostrich. The *náqa* ("Shadaníyyan mare") is attacked by a desert cat and veers aside from the pools of Dáylam. Water holes, normally a sign of security and renewal, are now pools of death. The episode of the "split-foot, long-nailed, stubby-ear" (the ostrich) carries equally somber associations. The comparison of the bird's wing carriage to a tent, a comparison that had been used by ʿAlqama in a playful manner, is here turned to a very different purpose: "like a funeral litter above a tented bier." The episode ends with another suggestion of mutilation, the ostrich, with its shaggy demeanor and earless head, likened to a "cut-eared, fur-draped slave."

In the long boast, reciprocal violence engulfs the voice of the poem.

Wine song turns to war song through an unusually immediate wine-blood analogy and the slaying of the drinker. The veil of the beloved is replaced by the armor of the warrior pierced and unseamed. The earlier reference to the "flash edge" of the beloved's teeth—the sword and tooth metaphor built upon the common trait of gleaming—is opened onto its more violent possibilities, as the image of bared teeth is reflected and refracted into the opponent's grin of terror, the mouth of the warrior's uncle giving him advice in the midst of war, the twisted grin of the horse in battle. The only reference to the *máysir* game, normally a sign of communal nourishment and unity, is cut short with the slaying of the *máysir* player. Generosity, normally a characteristic of the rains that are evoked by the remembrance of the beloved, or of the hero providing for the tribe, is transformed into the giving of a spear thrust and the feeding of desert predators with the remains of the enemy. The poetic voice turns in ever narrower circles. The last section of the ode consists of repeated images of the piercing of the opponent's armor and the abandonment of his body as carrion.

Speech is drowned. The spear is *summ* (hard, deaf, silent). The only voices are the gurgling of a wound, the muffled groan, the complaint the horse would make were it capable of speech. The only actual words, "ʿAntara, on!", are said to cure the hero's illness, but the cure is the disease, more of the same battle chaos. Once again an erotic motif, the reference (as in the ode of Dhu al-Rúmma) to the beloved as both the disease and the cure, finds a darker parallel in the boast.

Little by little a truth is unmasked. A hint had been given earlier, when ʿAntara described his opponent's neck wound as "twitching like the mouth of a harelip." In his biographical legend, it is ʿAntara who is described as a harelip. The cycle of reciprocal violence breaks down all difference between father and son, kin and non-kin, and, ultimately, self and other. Rather than the hierarchical relations upon which culture is based, there is a reflection of a single image, infinitely repeated as if in a set of doubled mirrors. The poem contains an unusual number of references to peers, brothers, and twins. These doublings are paralleled linguistically by a heavy use of grammatical duals and reduplicated lexical forms. The final occurrence of such doubling is ʿAntara's reference to the slaying of the father of the two sons of Dámdam (Dámdam itself being a reduplication of the word for union, and a reduplicated, partial echo of the word for blood). The hero's earlier words to the beloved cannot help but be recalled: "killing her kinsmen, coveting, by your father's life, what is not to be." In the context of mimetic doubling, the identity of the father becomes charged and ambivalent, and the identity of the love that was not to be "coveted" takes on a new possibility. At the moment of death in blood vengeance—a process of infinitely repeatable retaliation that can continue until both warring tribes are destroyed—the secret is unmasked: the hero looks into the death grin of his enemy and sees his peer, his twin, himself.

'Antara ibn Shaddād of the tribe of 'Abs is said to have lived in the sixth century C.E., to have been born to a slave of his father and later adopted into the father's full lineage, and to have fought in the War of Dāḥis. He later became the subject of the vast *Romance of 'Antar* (154 books in the 1868–93 Beirut edition), an oral epic that, though less well known in the West, has been as popular and influential as that other oral romance cycle, the *Arabian Nights*. For an account of the European discovery of a copy of the romance—ironically, on a mission to purchase a copy of the *Arabian Nights*—and the subsequent scholarship, see Peter Heath, "A Critical Review of Modern Scholarship on the *Sīrat 'Antar Ibn Shaddād* and the Popular *Sīra*," *Journal of Arabic Literature* XV (1984): 19–44.

Verses 59–62 (Tibrīzī's order), beginning with *yā shāta*, have been omitted as a probable interpolation.

The meter, like that of the Mu'allaqa of Labīd, is the *kāmil*. An unusual feature of this ode is the repetition of the *maṭla'*, or verse with an interior rhyme between hemistichs. The *maṭla'* is usually used only for the opening verse, but here each of the first two verses contains an interior hemistich rhyme. Verse 2:

　　－ － ◡ － / ◦ ◡ － 　◡ 　/ ◦ ◡ － ◡ －
　yā dāra 'ablata bi l-jiwā'i takallamī
　　　◡ ◡ － ◡ － / － － ◡ － / ◦ ◡ － 　◡ －
　wa 'imī ṣabāḥan dāra 'ablata wa slamī

Translator's divisions: the *nasīb*; the journey, with a brief horseback vignette, the *nāqa* ("Shadaniyyan mare"), and the ostrich ("split-foot, long-nailed, stubby-ear"); the warrior's boast.

The Muʿállaqa

Have the poets left anywhere
   in need of patching? Or did you,
after imaginings,
   recognize her abode?

        O abode of ʿAbla in al-Jiwáʾi,
     speak! Morning greetings,
        abode of ʿAbla,
     peace!

There I halted my camel mare,
   towering like a fortress above me—
to consummate the care
   of one who lingers.

        ʿAbla makes camp in al-Jawáʾi,
     while our tribe
        in al-Házni, then as-Suwán,
     then Mutaththálam . . .

Long live traces
   time made old,
barren and empty
   after Umm al-Háytham.

        She pitches camp
     in the land of the bellowers . . .
        hard for us, seeking
     you, Bint Mákhrami!

I fell for her by chance,
   killing her kinsmen,
coveting, by your father's life,
   what is not to be.

        You have come to rest—
     don't doubt me in it—
        at the way station
     of the honored beloved,

But where is the chance for our meeting,
   her people in ʿUnáyzatayn
following spring pastures,
   mine in Gháylam?

You had set your mind on parting,
   yes, but only on a night
      darkened in cloud
   were your mounts bridled,

The fear I felt, no more
   than the pack camels of her clan,
among the tents
   champing the Khímkhim berries,

      Twenty-four milch camels
      as black
         as the inner wing feathers
      of the blackest crow.

She takes your heart
   with the flash edge of her smile,
her mouth sweet to the kiss,
   sweet to the taste,

      As if a draft of musk
      from a spiceman's pouch
         announced the wet gleam
      of her inner teeth,

Fragrant as an untouched meadow,
   bloom and grass
sheltered in rain, untrodden,
   dung-free, hidden.

      Over it the white,
      first clouds of spring
         pour down, leaving small pools
      like silver dirhams,

Pouring and bursting,
   evening on evening
gushing over it
   in an endless stream.

      The fly has it all to himself,
      and is not about to leave,
         droning softly,
      like a wine drinker humming a tune,

Then buzzing, elbow on elbow,
   like a one-armed man
kindling a fire,
   bent down over the flint.

         At evening and at dawn she travels
         on a pillow
            while I spend the night
            on a bridled black stallion,

My cushion the saddle
   over his thick-legged,
full-flanked,
   barrel-girthed frame.

         Will a Shadaníyyan mare,
         shut off from nurslings,
            udders dry,
            carry me to her dwelling?

After a full night's journey
   still lashing her tail,
still strutting,
   smashing the sand mounds and pawing,

         As if one evening I were
         blasting through the sand mounds
            on a split-foot,
            long-nailed, stubby-ear,

Chicks skittering after
   like droves of Yemeni camels
flocking toward a foreigner
   who stammers and babbles.

         They follow the jug of his head
         as if they were following
            a funeral litter
            above a tented bier.

Knob-skulled, gawk-necked,
   he returns to his eggs
in Dhu ʿUsháyra, then stands
   like a cut-eared, fur-draped slave.

She watered at al-Duhrudáyn,
then veered,
forequarters pulling,
turning aside from the water holes of Dáylam,

As if she were pulling away
with her wild side
from a huge-headed
howler of the evening.

A dune cat that clings to her side,
warding her off
with teeth and claws
when she turns raging against it.

She kneels at the water
of al-Ridá'i
as if kneeling on broken-down,
dried-out, crackling reeds,

As if thick oil
or black pitch,
fit for kindling a blaze
around a heavy pot,

Streamed behind the ear
of a hot-tempered,
massive mare, strutting like a well-bred,
bite-scarred stallion.

If you let your veil down before me,
know that I am skilled
in seizing the horseman
in his coat of mail.

Praise me
as you knew me,
manner easy
until wronged.

Given wrong
I give it back,
rough as a taste
of bitterapple.

I am known
   when the hot hours calm
to be drinking wine,
   laying down a minted coin,

        A tawny luster
        from a goblet of banded glass
           near a gleaming pitcher
        stoppered on the windward side.

When drinking, all I own
   I spend away,
though what I am
   is undiminished.

        When sobered,
        I don't stop giving,
           true to nature
        as you have come to know me.

How many an unadorned beauty's lover
   have I left thrown flat,
jugular vein twitching
   like the mouth of a harelip.

        My hand beat him to it
        with a quick thrust,
           and a spray of blood
        the color of 'Andam crimson.

Why not ask your horsemen,
   daughter of Málik,
if what you do not know
   is beyond you?

        How I clung to the saddle
        of a surging stallion,
           a charger, wound-weary,
        taken on by warriors one on one,

Now in mid-field
   exposed for a run of the spear,
now drawn back
   behind an endless harvest of bows.

Let the battle witnesses
let you know
how I rush into the dust-roar blindly,
then hold back from the spoils.

How many a weapon-shrouded warrior,
whose approach is ruin,
inexperienced in fleeing
or surrender,

Have my hands awarded
the quick thrust
of a tempered, well-joined,
straightened spear,

Gashing him open,
the gurgling of his wound
guiding through the darkness
hunger-worn wolves in search of prey.

I split through his breastplate
with a hard, cold blade—
the spear tip holds inviolate
no stout-hearted brave—

and left him carrion
to be torn apart,
skull to wrist
by rustling predators.

And how many a coat of mail
on how many a famous
protector-of-his-own
has my sword unseamed.

How many a thrower of the gaming arrow,
in winter cold fast-handed,
captor of the tavern's banner,
ill reputed,

Upon seeing me dismounted,
searching him out,
has bared his molars
in what was not a smile.

I ran him through with a spear,
   then drove down
upon him with a whetted,
   unalloyed Indian sword.

      As the day spread out
      he lay before me,
        head and fingertips
      as if smeared with indigo dye,

A champion, when draped in armor,
   like the desert-dwarfing Sárha tree,
with hard-tanned oxskin boots,
   without twin.

      They tell me ꜥAmr
      is ungrateful for the gift
        I gave him. Thanklessness rots
      the soul of the giver.

Never will I forget
   my father's brother's
forenoon warning, lips pulled back
   from the flash of his mouth,

      As the whirl of death
      dragged champion after champion down,
        with no complaint
      but a swallowed groan.

Cut off by spear tips
   and held at bay,
I refused to turn back,
   my foot space narrowing.

      Then I heard Múrra's cry
      rising forth
        and the cry of the two sons of Rabíꜥa
      in the coagulating dust,

And Muhállim
   coming down on us
banners unfurled,
   death beneath the banners of Muhállim,

I knew that when they met us
there'd be a blow
    that would snap the nuzzled head
from a sleeping bird.

When I saw them all approaching,
  inciting one another on,
I wheeled about
  but incurred no blame.

        "'Antara!" they cried,
        their spears like well-ropes
          netting the forechest
        of my deep black stallion.

I hurled him,
  head-blaze and breast-pit,
again and again upon them
  until he was shirted with blood.

        With forequarters from the spear-fall
        twisting away,
          he complained to me
        through tears and snorting.

Had he known how to speak
  he would have protested.
Had he known to use words
  he would have let me know.

        Horses sank in the soft soil,
        mouths twisted into grins,
          long-bodied mares, and long-bodied
        short-haired stallions.

My soul was cured of its sickness
  and restored
by the cries of the horsemen,
  "'Antara, on!"

        Riding camels respond to my call.
        My heart is my companion.
        Wherever I wish to go
        I urge it on with a firm command.

I feared I would die
   before the wheel of war
turned down
   over the two sons of Dámdam

        Who slandered me
        though I never did them the same,
           vowing blood
        if I failed to meet them.

Let them—
   I left their father
carrion for the lion
   and the grey-faced bird of prey.

Al-Aʿsha

Bid Huráyra Farewell

In ʿAntara's poem, the erotic voice was engulfed in reciprocal violence. In this poem, it disguises itself in a dance of hyperbole. The self-mocking tone is set from the opening evocation of the beloved, with its exaggeration of conventional standards of beauty: tender walk, soft skin, narrow waist, lowered gaze, and dignified behavior. The depiction of Huráyra as a delicate lady reaches its extreme as she collapses in fatigue after a brief conversation with a neighbor.

The first part of the *nasíb* ends with a run of dissembling similes: perfume to the scent of musk and rose jasmine to the flooded garden. The second part of the *nasíb* parodies two more *nasíb* themes: the lover's complaint and the love-mad poet. An enumeration of mismatched lovers ends in confusion (the reader is advised not to sort out too closely the relationships at the end of the list), a confusion that echoes the lover's mental state. The bacchic mood gives way, suddenly, to a mention of fate ("intimations of death shades") that, as in most true bacchic movements, stands out in high relief from the proclaimed refusal to consider anything but the enjoyment of the moment.

The "intimations" verse might well have signaled the end of the *nasíb*, but Al-Aʿsha's ode luxuriates in an unhurried enjoyment of erotic themes. Accenting this lack of urgency is the confusion among various recensions concerning the order of verses. The linear progression is at times difficult to discern. Instead of a transition to a journey, there is a passage depicting a storm and wine-drinking, the desert earth and the drinkers both quenched. The thematic center of the passage is the poet's command to the drinkers: "Foretell!" (*shímu*). The foretelling of the rain's direction, the foretelling of the loss of the beloved and of the spring pasture grounds, and the premonition of mortality are brought together with semantic and metrical force in the one-word command. The actual act of foretelling consists of a recounting of the places upon which the rain might fall. This kind of litany usually occurs (as in Labíd's Muʿállaqa) in the *zaʿn* section of the *nasíb*, where the place names are the stations (*maqamát*) of the beloved's journey away from the poet. Here, by the poetic logic of association—the association of the beloved with rain and fertility—the clouds and rains take the place of the beloved, and it is their stations that are recounted.

The journey extends the parody as the poet declares himself to be shod at times and shoeless at others, a combination of two mutually exclusive movements: the journey of the tribal hero, accoutered and mounted on his camel mare, and the journey of the *suʿlúk*, the brigand, barefoot, traveling without mount, engaging in night raids. Defrayal and subversion of the journey continues as rhetorically grand phrases (the setting out at dawn for the journey or hunt, the mention of a companion, usually sword, spear, or bow) are turned to wine song. Only the last three verses (beginning with the "back of the shield" simile used also in the *Lámiyya* of Shánfara) are free of satirical play.

The poem ends with a missive boast: "To Yazíd of the Báni Shaybán bear this word." It is a powerful section built around a reference to the famous battle of the Bowbend, in which the poet's tribal confederation, the Bakr, defeated the Persians and their Arab allies. The fragility of linear perspective and verse order becomes especially acute in the boast. There is a high occurrence of textual variants and some hemistichs appear in more than one verse, a clear sign of textual instability. The breakdown of narrative closure and textual certainty—strong even by the standards of the oral, pre-Islamic tradition—is reflected by a similar breakdown of normal order in the battle. A woman, Futáyma, finds herself at the center of an attack, defended by the poet's tribe, rather than following the bedouin custom of watching the battle from a distance. A second woman, "the Jashiríyya," is mentioned within the context of battle taunts, but her role is never made clear. The enemy here turns out to be not so much the Persians, but the tribe of Abu Thubáyt which, like Al-Aʿsha's tribe, was part of the Bakr confederacy. Dissolution of normal boundaries of kin and enemy, self and other, is marked by an ever more urgent command to end the conflict, each command followed by the threat of more war. The use of parallelism becomes more dense, heightening the rhetorical intensity. At the moment of highest poetic pitch the poem refers to the enemy as that "tribe of ours" (*qáwmana*).

The missive boast and its distinctive version and vision of war, the vivid and textured imagery of the storm, and especially the appropriation of journey, hunt, and *suʿlúk* themes by the bacchic and erotic world of wine song have made this poem one of the most memorable and most loved of the classical odes. It inaugurates a satirical tradition that will last at least until Abu Nuwás, the ʿAbbasid wine poet celebrated for his night journey to the tavern, and his boasts of the power, nobility, and virtues (magical and heroic) of his wine.

Al-Aʿshā (the near-blind) was the nickname for Maymūn ibn Qays of the tribe of Bakr, clan of Qays ibn Thaʿlaba, who traveled widely, spent time at al-

Ḥīra, became famous for satires and wine songs, lived on into early Islam, and is said to have shown stubborn reluctance to embrace the new, wine-banning religion.

I have not included the disputed verses 51–53, which consist of a listing of the tribes of Banī Asad, Qushayr, ʿAbdallah, and Rabīʿa as witnesses to the fighting ability of the poet's tribe.

The meter, like that of the ode of ʿAlqama, is the *basīṭ*, with one important difference. In ʿAlqama, each hemistich ends with a spondee, while this ode uses an anapestic variant (˘ ˘ –). The anapest gives a metrical emphasis to the satire, as in the last hemistich of the first verse, where the lightness of the anapest in *rajulu* (man) contrasts, with comic effect, to the heavier feet and grand rhetoric of *ayyuhā* (O!), a contrast heightened further by the elision of the *hā* in *ayyuhā* with the trilled double *r* in *rajulu*:

```
 –   –        ˘ – / ˘ ˘   – / – – ˘   – /  ˘ ˘ –
waddiᶜ      hurayrata  inna r-rakba murtaḥilū
bid farewell to Huráyra, the riders are departing

 ˘   –      ˘ – / ˘ ˘ – / ˘      – ˘ – / ˘ ˘ –
wa hal     tuṭīqu wadāᶜan     ayyuhā r-rajulū
and can you  bear farewell, O    man (that you are).
```

A similar effect can be found in the next line with *muṣqûlun awāriḍuhā* (gleaming—her side teeth), the anapest giving an exaggerated emphasis to the long open *wā* in *awāriḍuhā*

Translator's divisions: first *nasīb* movement; second *nasīb* movement—the chain of mismatched lovers; the storm; the journey, *ṣuʿlūk* journey, and journey as wine song; missive boast.

Bid Huráyra Farewell

Bid Huráyra farewell.
  The riders are departing.
Can you, man that you are,
  bear bidding farewell?

      Brow aglow, hair flowing,
      a gleam from the side teeth as she smiles,
      she walks gently as a gazelle,
      tender-hoofed in wet soil,

As if her walk
  from the tent of a neighbor
were the gliding of a cloud
  neither slow nor hurried.

      You hear her anklets whisper
      as she turns away
      like cassia rustling
      suppliant in the breeze.

She's not one of those
  whose neighbors hate to see her face.
You won't find her,
  ear to their secrets, listening.

      She braces herself
      or she'd be thrown back flat,
      when rising to visit a neighbor,
      by languor.

She entertains her companion awhile,
  then slackens,
lower back and buttocks
  quivering,

      Full at the bodice,
      at the waist sash nil,
      a belle, seeming as she comes near
      to divide in two.

How sweet a bedmate
  on a cloudy afternoon,
not for some unbathed rude
  to lay and take some pleasure,

Wide-hipped, delicate,
    elbows soft, walk tender,
        as if a thorn were caught
    in the arch of her sandal.

As she rises
    a fragrance of musk trails,
her sleeve-cuffs with the scent
    of rose jasmine brimming over.

        No meadow of the meadows
    of the roughland plateau,
        luxuriant and green, blessed
    by dark-trailing big-dropped clouds,

Where the sun is teased
    by a blossom in full flower,
drenched in color,
    mantled deep in rushes and greens,

        Is ever more fragrant,
        more redolent
            than she, or more beautiful
        when evening shadows fall.

———————

Huráyra said
    when I came to pay her call
woe to you, woe,
    you woesome male!

        I fell for her by chance.
        She fell for another
            who fell for another
            other than her,

For him a girl was falling
    he didn't desire,
while a cousin on her father's side
    was weakening for her, and dying.

        Then for me there fell another,
        not to my liking,
            love in love on love,
            beside itself, entangled, mad,

Each of us afflicted,
    raving to this friend or that,
approaching, backing off,
    ensnared, ensnaring.

        Huráyra shut us off,
        not speaking,
            ignorance on the part of Umm Khuláyd
        of the bond she tied.

Didn't she see a man,
    night-blind, wounded
by intimations of death shades
    and by time, the demented, the undoing?

————————

        Have you seen it blocking the horizon?
        I passed the night in watch,
            lightning kindled along its edges,
        flickering,

With a dark trail behind it,
    its middle full and moving,
girded and held together
    by buckets of rain.

        No play diverts me
        from foretelling the rain's direction,
            no pleasure from a cup of wine,
        no languor.

I told them at Dúrna,
    the drinkers, already sodden:
Foretell! But how
    can a wine-faced drinker heed?

        Lightning lit up the slopes
        where the rain would fall,
            in Khabíyya, a blackening cloud
        against the horizon.

They said let it pour
    on Leopard Streak and Camel Belly,
on Horse Trappings, Tired Man,
    and Legland,

Flowing over the Edgelands,
  then Boar with its tracts
    of rock and sand,
      until the hills and mountains burst,

Until the grouse meadows
  and the tree-hedged
soft-curved dunes
  take all they can bear,

        A gushing, quenching draught
          for abodes long since desolate,
            off the track
              shunned by horse and camel mare.

You may well find me barefoot,
  not a scrap of shoe leather to my name.
Wearing boots or shoeless,
  that's the way I am.

        I might well steal upon
          some master of his house
            and catch him unawares. Wary once,
              now he finds no haven.

I might one day lead the reins
  of youthful passion,
and it might follow,
  a hot-blooded love-talker at my side.

        Many's the time I have set out at dawn
          to the wine shop,
            followed by a bob-skewing, quick-witted,
              path-wise fast-hander,

In a crowd of men like Indian swords
  who know that everyone,
barefoot or bootshod,
  will perish.

        I rivaled them down for the snip of basil,
          head on elbow, reclining,
            and for a tangy wine
              from a porous, moistened jug of clay.

They don't come to
   while there is any of it left,
except to call for more
   after a third round or after a second,

          The glass-bearer
          busying here and there,
             shirt bottom tucked up,
          alert, agile.

How many a song—you'd think it sung
   to a Persian harp—
when a singing girl in a nightslip
   sings it,

          How many a gowned lady,
          trailing silk,
             how many a girl
          with a leather wine flask at her side,

Have I spent my time enjoying,
   enduring trial
by amorous talk
   and length of pleasure.

          How many a land
          like the flat back of a shield,
             wild, where jinn are overheard
          in the corners, rustling,

That no one dares enter,
   riding upon the burning heat,
except one who, in what he undertakes,
   is unhurried,

          Have I cut through
          on a well-worn, rock-ribbed,
             easy-gaited mare, elbows well apart
          when you show her.

_____

To Yazíd of the Báni Shaybán
   bear this word:
Abu Thubáyt,
   stop gnawing at your heart!

Stop carving at the grain
of our ancient name
that nothing can harm
as long as burdened camels groan,

Like a mountain goat
butting against a rock
to split it, the rock unharmed,
the horns weakening.

I know you well
when the battle signal calls us,
when war blazes
with arms, night raids, and plunder.

You inflame Mas'úd's kin
and his brothers against us,
sowing destruction when we meet,
then drawing away.

Don't sit alone
when you've stoked the fire!
You'll implore refuge one day
from its burning, praying.

There were among the people of Kahf,
when they fought, and the Jashiríyya,
those who were quick,
those who would take their time.

You claimed we wouldn't fight you.
We are—tribe of ours!—
for the likes of you,
the killers,

Until the chief of the tribe
lies fallen, head on arm,
protected by child-bereft women's
flailing hands,

Struck down by an Indian sword
well aimed toward its target,
or a supple, well-tempered spear
from Khatt.

We might well spear the chieftain
in the hollow of his thigh,
and a champion might perish
on our spear tips, unavenged.

End it!
Nothing curbs the overbearing
like a gaping wound
unstaunched by oil and gauze.

By the life of the one
to whom stamping camels
and long-horned cattle of every kind
are led in offering,

Kill a chief
who never stood in your way
and we'll kill one of yours
like him, one to our choosing.

Try us. You won't find us
after the battle
from the tribe's blood-right
turning away.

Under the noon sun,
the day of the Bowbend,
around Futáyma, we were the riders,
not shirking, not giving way.

They called for a mounted attack.
We said we can do that.
They prepared to fight on foot.
We're a tribe that fights unmounted.

Dhu al-Rúmma

To the Encampments of Máyya

By the second century of Islam, the classical tradition of Arabic poetry was on the verge of a major change. Poetry was now composed in the new cities of Islam rather than in the deserts of the bedouin. The new religion, writing, philosophy, and the multicultural world of the city were among the converging pressures that were to bring about the first major transformation of the qasida.

The poetry of Ghaylán ibn ʿUqba, nicknamed Dhu al-Rúmma, marks the boundary of the ancient tradition. It remains close enough to the spirit of the bedouin qasida to have earned its author the title "seal of the classical poets." Yet it also reflects the turn to a new era. The words "desire" and "love" (háwa and hubb) appear far more frequently than in earlier poetry, for example. This direct expression of emotion is accompanied, paradoxically, by a new sense of indirection in syntax and diction. The verb káda ("nearly" or "almost" in verbal form) appears at moments of emotional intensity.

A combination of intensity and indirection is reflected in the poem's structure as well as in its language. Between the nasíb and the journey, there is a long section with three separate lines that could serve as a transition. In syntax, vocabulary, and imagery, the three are virtually identical. All refer to Máyya as being behind a veil of desert. The mention of the desert would normally mark the beginning of the journey, but in the first two cases the poet-hero slips back into remembrance of Máyya.

The existence of a critical space between the poet and the beloved is central to the poem, but the geographical positions of Máyya and the poet are undefined. There is only a vague reference to her changing the aim of her journey and to the condition of her abode. In the second case the emphatic "right there" (hátika) underlines the fact that we have no idea where "there" is. Nor do we know if the poetic persona is actually standing over the abode or only imagining himself to be there. The poet seems to lose himself in the temporal and spatial discontinuities that mark the nasíb-journey frontier.

Dislocation reaches its extreme when the rider, intoxicated from heat, mirage, and remembrance of Máyya, sways as if from the ropes of a well. Instead of a clearly defined past time and topography, there is only the memory of the beloved. Instead of a clearly defined intention or *hímma*, there is only a vague movement toward the lost past. Máyya becomes the beginning of the journey and the end—and the guide. Yet whenever the poet focuses his gaze upon her she vanishes. What at first seems to be a description of her turns into metamorphosis. She disappears into a landscape of wet dunes, desert torrents, deep abysses, camomile petals covered by night dew, and earth-soaked fragrance of the oasis breeze.

She is an affliction. Love for her is personified subtly, bringing to mind the *tayf*, the nightly apparition of the departed lover. This obsessional eroticism echoes the Medinan *'údhri* love poetry associated with Jamíl and Majnún Láyla, and foretells similar themes in the later Andalusian poetry of Ibn Zaydún and Ibn Khafája. In the final account it is the desert animals that are portrayed as existing with solidity. We leave the poem with clear images of the vulnerability of gazelle and fawn, the motion of the riding camels ("fleet roans"), the endurance of the "bite-scarred rough-flank" (onager), a glimpse of the "black-horn" (oryx bull), the monumental yet dynamic form of the *náqa*: the perduring world that preceded the life of the poet and will continue on after his death.

The poem ends not with a boast, but with a return to the remembrance of the beloved who is both disease and cure. She is many-guised (*dhátu alwánin*), an epithet that is the matrix of a rich set of associations. Time as fate (*dahr*) was called the many-guised, changing, wearing down all things, playing with human aspirations. The desert was many-guised, mirage-filled, leading the journeyer from tract into tract, devouring him. These meanings were personified in the *ghul*, that female jinni often called simply "the many-guised," the multiformed and changing-in-form beguiler of the desert traveler who leads him off the path to his destruction. Through the lightest and most subtle play upon this epithet the poet has evoked and united these associations. In the final complaint, the referent for "she-with-many-guises" is itself multivalent. The immediate antecedent is the beloved, but another antecedent is the mirage-filled desert of the journey, and, beyond that, fate. The term *dhátu alwánin* (she-with-many-guises) is also an inversion of the poet's nickname, *dhu al-rúmma* (he-with-a-cord-of-rope), the poet-hero attempting to bind the many-guised and constantly changing into a stable and secure world.

The end of the ode suggests that the transition to and through the journey has not been completed. There is no reintegration with tribal society. Dhu al-Rúmma, like the *su'lúk*, is passed from desert to desert, but rather than wandering ever further from the tribe, he wanders ever deeper into remembrance. By the end of the poem, the remembrance of the beloved and the journey, the temporal movement back through time and the journey across the spatial expanse of the desert, are one movement.

Dhū al-Rumma, one of the most famous of the poets of the Umayyad Caliphate, is said to have died *circa* 117 H./735 C.E., and to have taken part in the rivalry between the two poet-satirists, al-Farazdaq and Jarīr, and in the controversies between the grammatical schools of Basra and Kūfa. Ghaylān and Mayya (alternatively, Maī) are among the more famous pairs of lovers in the Arabic tradition. For a discussion of the ʿUdhrī tradition of love poetry, see Asʿad Khairallah, *Love, Madness, and Poetry: An Interpretation of the Majnūn Legend* (Beirut: Beiruter Texte und Studien, 1980).

The meter, like that of Shanfarā's *Lāmiyya*, is the *ṭawīl*:

  ᵕ   _ ᵕ / ᵕ _   _ _ / ᵕ _ _ / ᵕ _ ᵕ _

a manzilatay mayyin salāmun ʿalaykumā

  ᵕ _ _ / ᵕ _   _ _ / ᵕ _ ᵕ / ᵕ _ ᵕ _

ʿalā n-naʾyi wa n-nāʾī yawaddu wa yanṣaḥū

Translator's divisions: first *nasīb* section; second *nasīb* section—the metamorphosis; *nasīb*-journey transition; the *nāqa* Ṣaydah; the onager ("bite-scarred rough-flank"); conclusion.

To the Encampments of Máyya

To the encampments of Máyya,
  both of you,
a well-meant word
  and distant greeting:

      May the rain-star Arcturus
      be over you still . . .
        and the rains of the Pleiades,
        pouring down and spreading,

Though it was you
  who stirred a lover's
disheartened desire,
  until the eye shed

      Tears, yes, that nearly,
      on knowing a campsite as Máyya's,
      if not released,
      would have killed,

Though I was already nearing thirty
  and my friends had learned better
and good sense had begun
  to weigh down folly.

      When distance turns other lovers,
      the first premonition
      of loving Máyya
      will still be with me.

Nearness to her
  cannot impoverish desire,
nor distance, wherever she might be,
  run it dry.

      The inner whisper
      of memory,
      reminiscence of Máyya,
      is enough to bruise your heart.

Desires have their way,
  circulate freely,
but I can't see your share of my heart
  given away.

Though in parting some love
is effaced and disappears,
yours in me is made over
and compounded.

You came to mind
when a doe ariel passed us,
right flank turned to the camel mounts,
neck lowered,

A doe of the sands, earth-hued,
with a white blaze on the forehead
and the forenoon sun
clear upon her back.

She leaves her fawn
on a dune, a grassy dune
in Múshrif, the glance of her eye
gleaming around him,

Gazing at us as if we intended harm
where we would meet him,
approaching us,
then backing away.

She is her like, in shoulder,
neck and eye,
but Máyya is more radiant than she, still—
more beautiful.

After sleep she is languor
The house exudes her fragrance.
She adorns it
when she appears in the morning,

As if her anklets and ivory
were entwined around a calotrope
stopping the water's flow
in the bed of a wadi,

With buttocks like a soft dune
over which a rain shower falls
matting the sand
as it sprinkles down,

Her hair-fall
    over the lower curve of her back,
soft as the moringa's gossamer flowers,
    curled with pins and combed,

            With long cheek hollows
            where tears flow,
                and a lengthened curve at the breast sash
            where it crosses and falls.

You see her ear pendant
    along the exposed ridge of her neck,
swaying out,
    dangling over the abyss.

            With a red thornberry tooth-twig,
            fragrant as musk and Indian ambergris
                brought in in the morning,
            she reveals

Petals of a camomile
    cooled by the night
to which the dew has risen at evening
    from Ráma oasis,

            Wafting in on all sides
            with the earth scent of the garden,
                redolent as a musk pod
            falling open.

The white gleam of her teeth,
    her immoderate laugh,
almost, to the unhearing
    speak secrets.

            She is the cure, she the disease,
            memory of her, misgiving,
                desire dead
            were it not for the affliction of distance.

Far-flung!
    her tribe cut off
behind biting winds
    that scour the hard ground.

72

How many a crow,
cawing separation,
  like a highborn Nubian woman
  wailing the dead,

Has confirmed my foreboding,
  Máyya changing direction,
striking fire
  with the staff of parting.

  Let the spouse of Máyya weep
  that purebred camels kneel
    worn out at the end of night
    before the house of Mai.

Die miserably
  husband of Mai!
Hearts belonging to Máyya
  are free of blemish, pure.

  Had they left her a choice,
  she would have chosen well.
  One like Máyya does not belong
  with the likes of you.

As if I sleep on a bed of awls
  while her spouse sleeps,
stretched out,
  on a sandy hillock.

  When I say Máyya is near
  the desert stretches out,
    dust-hued,
    as far as the eye can see.

Mai has packed up and gone.
  Right there is her abode!
Left to the limping crow
  and ring-necked dove.

  When I complained to Máyya of love
  that she might reward me
    for my affections, she said:
    You're not being serious!

Keeping me off,
   leading me on,
when she saw that the specter of love
   had almost made off with my body.

———————

       How many a noonday heat,
       far from Mai,
          the pace of my thick-humped mare unbroken,
       the black-white locusts twitching

In pathless wastelands
   whose stillness
in the mirage of forenoon and midday
   almost blots out the gaze,

       As if the flat hill summits
       were entwined in pure silk
          parting at times to reveal them,
       then sewed back,

When the chameleon
   struck by the heat
begins to twist his head
   and reel—

       How many a rider
       drunk on sleeplessness
          as if swaying from the two ropes
       of a concave well

Have I shaken from his stupor
   as he nodded his head
like a staggering drinker
   after his last drop of wine.

       When he expires in the saddle
       I bring him back to life
          with your memory. The fleet roans
       lean to their gallop.

When the end of the whip frays
   and the bodies of the camels
are worn to sickles
   then Sáydah besets them.

She has stubby ears
and a long upper nape,
a cheek polished
like the mirror of a foreign lady,

The eyes of a black-horn,
solitary,
lips like Yemeni leather
that flap loosely when she paces,

A leg like the shadow of a wolf,
stride met
by the lower foreleg
twisted out wide by the shinbone,

At full gallop
when the black of night
is parted from the riders
by the pale horizon of dawn.

When I call out "aaj!"
or intone the camel driver's song
she lifts a tail like under-wing feathers
as if pregnant or false-pregnant.

You see her
when I have imposed upon her
every hardship, before the trail camels,
their forelegs pulling in air,

Her legs surging,
body lunging,
wary of threats,
head raised,

Tawny, towering,
as if a bite-scarred rough-flank
bore me in the saddle
through the empty regions.

He turns the herd,
driving and urging, their flanks
like boulder-strewn ground
in a field of brush grass.

They grazed dry pastures
   until they became as thin
as well-straightened spear shafts
   from Khatt.

        Until there came a day
      when in their sand hollows
        ostrich eggs
      nearly split in the blaze.

He continued to beguile them,
   as they stood, thirst-parched,
as if on the crowns of their heads
   were a flock of birds,

        On a promontory
      at the dust hour
        when locusts expire
      from the force of heat.

You see the wind play
   where she travels at nightfall
between her and what she will find
   where she arrives at dawn.

        As if the camels
      through the far-flung, trackless barrens
        were boats floating
      in the desert of the Tigris.

My heart refused everything
   but memory of Máyya.
She-with-many-guises, playful and serious,
   troubled it.

Glossary

Arabic terms are given first with English accents and then with formal, Arabic transliteration, based upon vowel quantity.

ahwál (aḥwāl): conditions, stances, or moods; the shifting moods or attitudes of the beloved vis-à-vis the lover.

atlál (aṭlāl): the abodes, marks, and traces of the beloved's abandoned campsite.

balíyya (baliyya): the ghost mare, the fallen hero's *náqa*, tethered to his tomb and abandoned.

dhikr (dhikr): remembrance, of the beloved, of one's relationship with the divine (Qurʾanic), of the divine beloved (Sufi).

diwán (dīwān): the collection of poetry ascribed to a single author.

fakhr (fakhr): the boast, the third major movement of the qasida, often including wine song, *náqa* sacrifice, depiction of the poet-hero on horseback, battle-boast and tribal boast.

ghul (ghūl): a female species of jinn associated with constant change of form, the changing moods of the beloved, the changing patterns of the desert that devour the traveler, the changes of time that wear down and wear away aspirations. The hair-covered, grave-robbing *ghul* of the Arab folktale tends to be male, more stable in form, easier to please than the *ghul* of poetry.

hilm (ḥilm): foresight, self-command, trail sense, ability to follow through on plans; the primary pre-Islamic virtue.

jahl (jahl): the opposite of *hilm*; the uncontrolled jumping of a young horse; recklessness, impetuosity, the tendency to take on endeavors, conflicts, or relationships unprepared. Pre-Islamic Arabia was called by early Muslims the *jahilíyya* (age and place of *jahl*), with *jahl* transformed into the sense of moral and religious ignorance.

jinni, pl. jinn (jinnī, jinn): semi-spirits of the desert, associated with love, madness, and poetic inspiration.

karím (karīm): an untranslatable term usually rendered as "generous" or "noble": the centerpiece of tribal ethos, symbolized through the *náqa* sacrifice and the feeding of the tribe, the unflinching defense of the clan in battle, the lavish wine bouts and banquets, and, in a more

77

abstract sense, the refusal to hoard one's life. The Qurʾan gave the *karím* a more ethical and religious dimension, but maintained its centrality as a human ideal.

maqamát (maqāmāt): stations of a journey; stations of the beloved's journey away from the poet.

máysir (maysir): a ritual lottery played with arrow shafts through which the slaughtered *náqa* is apportioned; a game with symbolic associations concerning fate.

muʿallaqát (muʿallaqāt): the "suspended ones," a famous collection of poetry, with various versions comprising between seven and ten poems. Legend maintains that they were hung from the walls of the pre-Islamic Kaʿba after poetry competitions at the fair of ʿUkáz.

náqa (nāqa): the camel mare, the poet-hero's mount during the journey and sacrificial victim during the major pre-Islamic rite, the *náqa* sacrifice. The *náqa* is almost always referred to through epithets ("the journey worn," "the Shadaníyyan," "the night courser," etc.).

nasíb (nasīb): remembrance of the lost beloved, the first section of the qasida.

onager: the Arabian species of wild ass, a major symbolic figure in the qasida, almost always mentioned by epithet ("sheen-of-udder," "white-belly," "bite-scarred rough-flank").

oryx: the white Arabian oryx (now being reintroduced to Arabia after several centuries of extinction). This particularly elegant species of antelope with long cylindrical horns becomes a central symbolic figure in the qasida, almost always mentioned through epithets ("wide-of-eyes," "wild one," "flat-nosed one").

rahíl (raḥīl): the journey, the second major movement of the qasida.

sirr (sirr): secret or mystery; the secret of the beloved-lover relation; the secret or mystery of destiny; the mystery of the divine being (Qurʾanic); one's interior, unmanifest, real self (Sufi).

suʿlúk (ṣuʿlūk): a brigand or outcast; a particular kind of qasida composed in the voice of the brigand.

tayf (ṭayf): the beloved's night apparition to the poet.

zaʿn (ẓaʿn or dhaʿn): the departure of the beloved and the women in her tribe and the depiction of their howdahs, the richly decorated litters carried on camel stallions.

Wesleyan Poetry in Translation

from Arabic

Desert Tracings: Six Classic Arabian Odes by ʿAlqama, Shánfara, Labíd, ʿAntara, Al-Aʿsha, and Dhu al-Rúmma. 1989. Translated and introduced by Michael A. Sells.

from Bulgarian

Because the Sea Is Black: Poems of Blaga Dimitrova. 1989. Translated and with introductions by Niko Boris and Heather McHugh.

from Chinese

Bright Moon, Perching Bird. 1987. The poems of Li Po and Tu Fu, translated and with an introduction by J. P. Seaton and James Cryer.

from Czechoslovakian

Mirroring: Selected Poems of Vladimir Holan. 1985. Translated by C. G. Hanzlicek and Dana Hábová.

from French

Fables from Old French: Aesop's Beasts and Bumpkins. 1982. Translated and with a preface by Norman Shapiro, introduction by Howard Needler.

The Book of Questions (Vols. I–VII in four books). 1976 to 1984. By Edmond Jabès. Translated by Rosmarie Waldrop.

The Book of Dialogue. 1987. By Edmond Jabès. Translated by Rosmarie Waldrop.

from German

Sonnets to Orpheus. 1987. The poems of Rainer Maria Rilke, translated and with an introduction by David Young.

from Italian

The Coldest Year of Grace: Selected Poems of Giovanni Raboni. 1985. Translated by Stuart Friebert and Vinio Rossi.

from Lithuanian

Chimeras in the Tower: Selected Poems of Henrikas Radauskas. 1986. Translated by Jonas Zdanys.

from Navajo

Hogans: Navajo Houses and House Songs. 1980. Translated by David and Susan McAllester.

from Portuguese

An Anthology of Twentieth-Century Brazilian Poetry. 1972. Edited and with an introduction by Elizabeth Bishop and Emanuel Brasil.

Brazilian Poetry, 1950–1980. 1983. Edited by Emanuel Brasil and William Jay Smith.

When My Brothers Come Home: Poems from Central and Southern Africa. 1985. Edited by Frank Mkalawile Chipasula.

from Serbian

Roll Call of Mirrors: Selected Poems of Ivan V. Lalić. 1988. Translated by Charles Simic.

from Spanish

Times Alone: Selected Poems of Antonio Machado. 1983. Translated and with an introduction by Robert Bly.

With Walker in Nicaragua and Other Early Poems, 1949–1954. The poems of Ernesto Cardenal, translated by Jonathan Cohen.

Off the Map: Selected Poems of Gloria Fuertes. 1984. Edited and translated by Philip Levine and Ada Long.

About the author

In 1972, Michael Sells went to Tunisia to teach English for the Peace Corps. During the next three years, he learned the Tunisian dialect and was deeply influenced by Arab culture. In 1976, he began studies in Arabic literature at the University of Chicago, interspersed with a year in Cairo, where he was introduced to the classical tradition of Arabic poetry at the Center for Arabic Studies Abroad. He won an American Association of Teachers of Arabic prize in both 1981 and 1982 for his first translations of Arabic qasidas, and, in 1985, a Columbia University Translation Center award for literary translation from the Arabic. He received a National Endowment for the Humanities summer fellowship to complete this, his first, book. He has published a number of articles and book reviews and is at work on two books of scholarship.

Sells was graduated from Gonzaga University, in Washington (A.B. 1971), and from the University of Chicago (Ph.D. 1982). He was Andrew W. Mellon postdoctoral fellow in the humanities at Stanford from 1982 to 1984. Since 1984 he has been assistant professor of Islam and comparative religions at Haverford College. He has been poetry editor for the *Chicago Review.* His home is in Haverford, Pennsylvania.

About the book

Desert Tracings was composed in Trajanus by Brevis Press of Bethany, Connecticut. This book was designed and produced by Kachergis Book Design, Inc. of Pittsboro, North Carolina.

Wesleyan University Press, 1989